D0031017

SPEAKING OF
BASEBALL

SPEAKING OF

BASEBALL

Edited by David Plaut

Running Press
Philadelphia, Pennsylvania

Copyright © 1993 by David Plaut. All rights reserved under the Pan-American and International Copyright Conventions.

The author gratefully acknowledges Black Literary Agency for permission to include extensive extracts from *Dodger Dogs to Fenway Franks* by Bob Wood, copyright © 1988 by Bob Wood.

This book may not be reproduced in whole or in part in any form or by any means, electronic or mechanical, including photocopying, recording, or by any information storage and retrieval system now known or hereafter invented, without written permission from the publisher.

Canadian representatives: General Publishing Co., Ltd., 30 Lesmill Road, Ontario M3B 2T6.

International representatives: Worldwide Media Services, Inc., 30 Montgomery Street, Jersey City, New Jersey 07302.

9 8 7 6 5 4 3 2 1

Digit on the right indicates the number of this printing.

ISBN 1–56138–238–8

Library of Congress Cataloging-in-Publication Number 92–50793

Edited by Gregory C. Aaron
Cover design by Toby Schmidt
Interior design by Christian Benton
Picture Research by Elizabeth Broadrup

Polaroid transfer process on all photos by Steve Belkowitz Photography. Front cover photo © UPI/Bettman. Back cover photo © D. Corson/H. Armstrong Roberts. Interior photos: pages 15, 55, 199, 269, 340, 360, 397 © UPI/Bettman; page 34 © D. Corson/H. Armstrong Roberts; pages 73, 94, 226, 313, 389 © FPG International; page 119 © Mike Valeri/FPG International; page 141 courtesy National Baseball Library, Cooperstown, N.Y.; pages 161, 245, 283 © Otto Greule Jr./Allsport USA; page 180 © AP/Wide World Photos; page 219 courtesy National Baseball Hall of Fame and Museum, Cooperstown, N.Y.

Typography: Gill Sans, with Arcadia and Insignia, by Richard Conklin.
Printed in the United States by Berryville Graphics

This book may be ordered from the publisher. Please add $2.50 for postage and handling. *But try your bookstore first!*

Running Press Book Publishers
125 South Twenty-second Street
Philadelphia, Pennsylvania 19103

To Joan and Jonathan,
the slickest double-play
combo in the game.

CONTENTS

Introduction 9

Baseball America 13

The Rite of Spring 25

Sandlots 33

A Dozen Great Baseball Nicknames 43

The Gathering Crowd 47

The Old Ballpark 60

What to Take to a Game 69

Bat on Ball 72

Glove Story 86

Circling the Bases 98

Big-Screen Baseball 106

Batterymates 113

Playing to Win 139

A Dozen Bizarre Baseball Injuries 152

The Man in the Dugout 155

The Boys in Blue 172

Bending the Rules 183

The Press Box 190

Five Books That Changed Baseball Writing 204

You Can Look It Up 210

Fifty Amazing Real Names of Major-League Players 217

The Business of Baseball 220

The Tenth Inning 235

Baseball Geography: The American League 243

Baseball Geography: The National League 270

All-Time Franchise All-Star Teams 292

Like No Other Sport 298

Then and Now 306

October's Game 317

The Five Biggest World Series Upsets 325

Diamond Twilight 329

The Five Saddest Days in Baseball 338

Legends of Cooperstown 342

Five Who Belong in the Hall of Fame 380

Life and Baseball 385

Index 399

INTRODUCTION

Once upon a time, baseball was America's favorite sport. These days, when fans are polled on the subject, football is usually the most popular choice. Telephone surveys and television ratings — the numbers — confirm this preference. The words, however, tell us that baseball was, and will always be, king.

More has been spoken and written about baseball than any other sport. The reasons go beyond its longevity. Baseball is the one game above all others that encourages both lengthy, leisurely writing side-by-side with rapid, caustic remarks. Baseball is a sport that takes its time, its pace inviting careful thought, substantive analysis . . . and lacerating insults that are the verbal equivalent to a custard pie in the face.

Check your library or neighborhood bookstore and compare the number (and quality) of baseball books with those on football, hockey, or tennis. Try to track down anthologies about basketball or skiing. The other sports may equal baseball in power, grace, and athleticism. Not one, however, comes close to baseball's prolific — and prosaic — body of words.

Baseball is names and dates and events and statistics. But beyond the data are the voices of the game — the observations, witticisms, crude remarks, and expressive quotations that put flesh and blood on the dry bones of final standings and box scores.

In the pages that follow, you'll find quotes, quips, poetry, and pomposities, alternately humorous and downcast, universal in scope, and self-serving. Here are more than a thousand quotations on everything that is baseball, accompanied by lists and short essays to amuse, annoy, and initiate arguments.

These are excerpts from the most expansive diary in sports, the verbal diamonds of a 150-year-old game ... these are the voices of baseball.

EDITOR'S NOTE

Each quote in this book is followed by the name of the person to whom the words are attributed, along with an appropriate affiliation and year reference.

If the person is a writer, the book, story, newspaper, or periodical in which his or her quote appears is identified, along with the year the piece was written. Where notable, the writer's year of birth (and death, where applicable) is included.

In the cases of players, managers, front office staff, and coaches, the identifying teams and seasons have been provided to: 1) pinpoint the exact year in which the quote was spoken, or 2) pair the quote with the team and era most appropriate with its content.

During their careers, many people in this book were affiliated with more than one franchise. For the sake of brevity, the most germane affiliation has been selected for each quote. That's why, for example, you'll find Casey Stengel identified as the Yankees manager in some places, and as the Mets manager in others.

BASEBALL AMERICA

I see great things in baseball. It's our game — the American game. It will take our people out of doors, fill them with oxygen, give them a larger physical stoicism. Tend to relieve us from being a nervous, dyspeptic set. Repair these losses, and be a blessing to us.

—Walt Whitman (1819–92)
poet

Baseball has remained The Game in modern America, and is still the American paradigm of team sports. Its initiates are participants. Whether they play or watch, the ritual is so involving, so real, so significant, that it colors and affects and explains and organizes the lives of its participants and of their communities.

—James Oliver Robertson
American Myth, American Reality (1980)

Think of the weddings that take place at home plate, the children who are named after heroes. Why? I don't know why, except what better thing is there to talk about? What common denominator do we have in this country that is better than baseball?

—Al Rosen
Indians third baseman (1947–56)

A baseball club is part of the chemistry of the city. A game isn't just an athletic contest. It's a picnic, a kind of town meeting.

—Michael Burke
Yankees president (1967–73)

A guy who's played one game in the pros is like a former state senator, a big man in most neighborhoods and any saloon as long as he lives.

—Wilfrid Sheed
"Diamonds Are Forever" (1985)

Any schnook can play it, and they do play it, at all levels, whether it is stickball in the streets or rockball in the country.

—Carlton Fisk
Red Sox catcher (1969, '71–80)

The '89 Oakland A's celebrate the supreme baseball
moment—the winning of the World Series championship.

Baseball? Just a game, as simple as a ball and a bat. And yet as complex as the American spirit it symbolizes. A sport, business and sometimes almost even a religion.

—Ernie Harwell
Tuned to Baseball (1985)

It is an American institution and more lasting than some marriages, war, Supreme Court decisions and even major depressions.

—Art Rust
Recollections of a Baseball Junkie (1985)

Baseball seems to exist under a bell jar, oblivious and impervious to the stresses of the world outside. With America's institutions under assault from all directions, baseball remains a world unto itself with its small, slow changes arising only from its own mandate.

—John Thorn and Peter Palmer
The Hidden Game of Baseball (1984)

Next to religion, baseball has furnished a greater impact on American life than any other institution.

—*Herbert Hoover (1874–1964)*
31st President of the United States

Baseball was here with stiff collars and bustles, before the motor car, after man's landing on the moon. No other spectator sport in America has meant so much to so many for so long.

—*Ira Berkow*
"The Smell of the Ball" (1973)

Baseball reflected the language of America, and spiced it, too. Presidents, politicians, executives, generals and parents touched all the bases regularly so that nobody would be out in left field or caught off base in the greater pursuits of life. If you did it right, you hit a grand slam home run; if not, you struck out.

—*Joseph Durso*
Baseball and the American Dream *(1986)*

It is the sport that a foreigner is least likely to take to. You have to grow up playing it, you have to accept the lore of the bubble gum card, and believe that if the answer to the Mays–Mantle–Snider question is found, then the universe will be a simpler and more ordered place.

—*David Halberstam (b. 1934)*
author

Whoever wants to know the heart and mind of America had better learn baseball.

—*Jacques Barzun*
"God's Country and Mine" (1954)

Baseball is democracy in action; in it all men are "free and equal," regardless of race, nationality or creed. Every man is given the rightful opportunity to rise to the top on his own merits. . . . It is the fullest expression of freedom of speech, freedom of press, and freedom of assembly in our national life.

—*Francis Trevelyan Miller*
Introduction to Connie Mack's My 66 Years in Baseball (1950)

It has been said that baseball is to the United States what revolutions are to Latin America, a safety valve for letting off steam. I think baseball is more serious than any Latin American revolution. But then, I am a serious fan.

—George Will
"Don't Beep in My Outfield" (1985)

Baseball reflects American society's need for confrontation.

—W.J. Weatherby
Manchester Guardian *(1988)*

Love America and hate baseball? Hate America and love baseball? Neither is possible, except in the abstract.

—John Krich
"El Beisbol" (1989)

To be an American and unable to play baseball is comparable to being a Polynesian and unable to swim. It's an impossible situation.

—John Cheever
"The National Pastime" (1953)

It's a Little Leaguer's game that major leaguers play extraordinarily well, a game that excites us throughout adulthood. The crack of the bat and the scent of the horsehide on leather bring back our own memories that have been washed away with the sweat and tears of summers long gone . . . even as the setting sun pushes the shadows past home plate.

—Mario Cuomo (b. 1932)
Governor of New York

Baseball is made up of very few big and dramatic moments, but rather it's a beautifully put together pattern of countless little subtleties that finally add up to the big moment, and you have to be well-versed in the game to truly appreciate them.

—Paul Richards
Orioles manager (1955–61)

Baseball, almost alone among our sports, traffics unashamedly and gloriously in nostalgia, for only baseball understands time and treats it with respect. The history of other sports seems to begin anew with each generation, but baseball, that wondrous myth of twentieth century America, gets passed on like an inheritance.

—Stanley Cohen
The Man in the Crowd *(1981)*

It can retain the romantic quality of the 19th century while the country hurtles pell-mell into the 21st. The men who play the game remain dream weavers.

—*Phil Hersh*
Chicago Tribune *(1985)*

The baseball past is a world the establishment can't touch. They can't cheapen it. They can expand, play on plastic, add wild-card teams to the playoffs, have a DH for every position, start the World Series on Christmas Day, or play the whole season in a television studio in Japan, but the lords of baseball and television moguls can't hurt the past.

—*Luke Salisbury*
The Answer Is Baseball *(1989)*

The baseball season — six months — 2,106 games — is flat out long, and it's a rare one of those games that doesn't ramble or sputter or digress or somehow (as they say in Lit class) violate the rules of dramatic narrative. Baseball takes its own sweet time reaching its conclusions.

—*Dwight Allen*
"Reds, Yanks and O's" *(1989)*

Baseball is overrated . . . I have lapped up all the propaganda about baseball being pastoral — whatever that is — and how, through baseball, we poor, uprooted Americans return to our rural pasts ever so briefly. Personally, I never had a rural past nor did any of my friends. In fact, most of the people who praise baseball because of that rural past baloney grew up in big cities and loved the sound of traffic and people arguing.

—Lowell Cohn
San Francisco Chronicle *(1982)*

By its nature, the watching of baseball appeals most strongly to imaginative people. The average major league games last approximately two hours and forty-five minutes. There is action for perhaps fifteen minutes of that time. The rest is either inaction or suspense, depending on imagination and point of view.

—Roger Kahn
"Intellectuals and Ballplayers" (1957)

It's just throwing and catching and hitting and running. What's simpler than that?

—Paul Richards
Orioles manager (1955–61)

I love baseball. It's given me everything I have. Look, there are only about six hundred major leaguers in the country. You have to feel special.

—Thurman Munson
Yankees catcher (1969–79)

Playing baseball for a living is like having a license to steal.

—Pete Rose
Reds infielder (1963–78, '84–86)

If they said, "Come on, here's a steak dinner," and I had a chance to go out and play a game of ball, I'd go out and play the game and let the steak sit there. I would.

—Lefty Grove
Athletics pitcher (1925–33)

It was just a game, that's all it was. They didn't have to pay me. I'd have paid them to let me play. Listen, the truth is it was more than fun. It was heaven.

—Goose Goslin
Senators outfielder (1921–30)

The sport to which I owe so much has undergone profound changes . . . but it's still baseball. Kids still imitate their heroes on playgrounds. Fans still ruin expensive suits going after foul balls that cost five dollars. Hitting streaks still make the network news. And the hot dogs still taste better at the ballpark than at home.

—Duke Snider
Dodgers outfielder (1947–62)

Baseball's future? Bigger and bigger! Better and better! No question about it — it's the greatest game there is!

—Ted Williams
Red Sox outfielder (1939–42, '46–60)

THE RITE OF SPRING

The game wakes gradually, gathering vigor in itself as the days lengthen late in February and grow warmer, old muscles grow limber, young arms throw strong and wild, legs pivot and leap, bodies hurdle into bright bases safe. . . . Migrating north with the swallows, baseball and the grass' first green enter Cleveland, Kansas City, Boston . . . so the diamonds and the rituals of baseball create an elegant, trivial, enchanted grid on which our suffering, shapeless, sinful day leans for the momentary grace of order.

—Donald Hall
"Baseball and the Meaning of Life" (1985)

In the beginning, there was no baseball. But ever since there have been few beginnings as good as the start of a new baseball season. It is the most splendid time in sport.

—*B.J. Phillips*
Time (1981)

Is there anything that can evoke spring . . . better than the sound of the ball smacking into the pocket of the big mitt, the sound of the bat as it hits the horsehide; for me . . . almost everything I know about spring is in it — the first leaf, the jonquil, the maple tree, the smell of grass upon your hands and knees, the coming into flower of April.

—*Thomas Wolfe*
You Can't Go Home Again (1940)

It is true that spring baseball makes millions more promises than it keeps. But baseball is unlike love. In baseball, making promises means vastly more than keeping them. Baseball promises, like records, are made to be broken. The promise is all that counts.

—*Edwin Pope*
"Baseball Spring" (1987)

From now into October, there will be games every day, athletes with faces and personalities . . . tomorrow there will be enough box scores and probable pitchers to read right through lunch. This is real life, starting today.

—George Vecsey
A Year in the Sun *(1989)*

People ask me what I do in winter when there's no baseball. I'll tell you what I do. I stare out the window and wait for spring.

—Rogers Hornsby
Cardinals infielder (1915–26)

In winter, I got cabin fever bad. I wish I had a tape recording of the sounds of batting practice.

—Ray Miller
Orioles pitching coach (1978–85)

The sound of the bat is the music of spring training. It runs like a fugue through the lives of the players and the fans, brightening the day with memories and associations . . . in the physics of baseball, this is the central collision, the origin of life.

—William Zinsser
Spring Training *(1989)*

Spring training is like a cat with nine lives. A baseball player has x number of lives and each spring is the birth of a new life.

—*Steve Garvey*
Dodgers infielder (1969–82)

Spring is the time of year when the ground thaws, trees bud, the income tax falls due — and everybody wins the pennant.

—*Jim Murray*
Los Angeles Times *(1965)*

During spring training . . . the local Chamber of Commerce will throw a barbecue for the big-leaguers and only three regulars will show . . . four players will tell the GM to "play me or trade me" . . . three pitchers will observe that the ball is a lot livelier this spring . . . two rookies will be hospitalized for severe sunburn . . . the record machine will break down during the playing of the national anthem.

—*Ernie Harwell*
Tuned to Baseball *(1985)*

I love going to spring training because it seems like baseball in its purest sense, the same game we played as kids. The scores don't mean anything; no one cares about the standings. It's just the game that matters.

—Pete Franklin
You Could Argue But You'd Be Wrong *(1988)*

No one's gonna give a damn in July if you lost a game in March.

—Earl Weaver
Orioles manager (1968–82, '85–86)

Watching a spring training game is as exciting as watching a tree form its annual ring.

—Jerry Izenberg
Newark Star Ledger *(1981)*

It's the fans that need spring training. You gotta get 'em interested. Wake 'em up. Let 'em know that their season is coming, the good times are gonna roll.

—Harry Caray (b. 1920)
Cubs broadcaster

No civilization that has produced baseball spring training can be all bad.

—*Leonard Koppett*
The New Thinking Fan's Guide to Baseball *(1991)*

Hope rises each spring like sap in the trees. That's part of baseball, that's one of the greatest things about the game. You have the annual rebirth no matter how disastrous the previous year was.

—*Harry Dalton*
Brewers general manager (1978–)

A young ballplayer looks on his first spring training trip as a stage-struck young woman regards the theatre. She can think only of the lobster supper and the applause.

—*Christy Mathewson*
Giants pitcher (1900–16)

I got the sophomore jinx out of the way and I think I'll have my best year ever next year. There's no junior jinx, is there?

—*Joe Charboneau*
Indians outfielder (1980–82)

What a player does best he should practice least. Practice is for problems.

—*Duke Snider*
Dodgers outfielder (1947–62)

People who write about spring training not being necessary have never tried to throw a baseball.

—*Sandy Koufax*
Dodgers pitcher (1955–66)

The only thing running and exercising can do for you is make you healthy.

—*Mickey Lolich*
Tigers pitcher (1963–75)

When I played, you came to spring training with a ten-pound winter beer belly on, and you ran about thirty wind sprints and you sweated with a sweat jacket and you got yourself in condition. Now the players do Nautilus all winter, they play racquetball, they swim, they exercise and they come to spring training looking like Tarzan.

—*Jim Leyland*
Pirates manager (1986–)

This is the best time of the year. Heck, once the season starts, I go to work.

—Brooks Robinson
Orioles third baseman (1955–77)

Soon enough the media would age these boys beyond their years by harping on their contracts and their agents, their sulks and their scrapes and their sore arms. But for six weeks in February and March they were allowed to be what they were: young men who played a wonderful game wonderfully well.

—William Zinsser
Spring Training *(1989)*

SANDLOTS

You gotta be a man to play baseball for a living, but you gotta have a lot of little boy in you.

—Roy Campanella
Dodgers catcher (1948–57)

Kids are always chasing rainbows, but baseball is a world where you can catch them.

—Johnny Vander Meer
Reds pitcher (1937–49)

Doctors tell me I have the body of a 30-year-old. I know I have the brain of a 15-year-old. If you've got both, you can play baseball.

—Pete Rose
Reds infielder (1963–78, '84–86)

There are no final outs in a neighborhood ballgame—
only Mom's call for dinner.

Boys would be big leaguers, as everybody knows, but so would big leaguers be boys.

—Philip Roth
The Great American Novel *(1973)*

The essence of the professional game in the United States of America is a small boy looking with absolute rapture at a grown man.

—Robert Creamer
Babe: The Legend Comes to Life *(1974)*

I won't be happy until we have every boy in America between the ages of six and sixteen wearing a glove and swinging a bat.

—Babe Ruth
Yankees outfielder (1920–34)

I was always too busy a boy to indulge in baseball.

—Thomas Edison (1847–1931)
inventor

Growing up, I never thought of playing pro ball. I wanted to do something meaningful — I wanted to be a surfer.

—Greg Minton
Giants pitcher (1975–87)

If you put a baseball and other toys in front of a baby, he'll pick up a baseball in preference to the others. The American boy starts swinging the bat as soon as he can lift one.

—Tris Speaker
Indians outfielder (1916–26)

To a toddler, a soft rubber ball is a friendly object, an inviting toy. When a youngster first encounters a baseball, however, and receives his baptismal bruise, he learns that this particular ball may be his enemy and he had better stay out of its path.

—John Thorn
The Game for All America (1988)

I've umpired everything and Little League is the toughest . . . the boys are so unpredictable. There's no telling where these kids will run, where they'll throw, what they'll do. That's what makes it fun.

—Tom Hunter
Little League umpire (1976)

Little League baseball is a much-maligned institution at the mercy of any psychiatrist in search of a headline. For him, it usually comes out as a combination of Hitler Youth and child labor and they usually recommend a constitutional amendment to ban it in favor of something they called "unstructured play."

—Jim Murray
Los Angeles Times (1973)

I look at my own kids, and the only time they play is in an organized league. Don't you learn more about something if you do it because you love it? Now it's just another kind of piano practice.

—Tom Grieve
Rangers general manager (1984–   )

I cannot agree with critics who claim there is too much stress put on the Little Leagues. To me, this is so much hokum. Boys must have the spirit of competition in some way and there is none better than baseball.

—Joe Cronin (1906–84)
American League President

The most important thing our Little League had was equipment. We were so tickled with our uniforms that we would show up for a 6:30 twilight game at about noon.

—Bob Turley
Yankees pitcher (1955–62)

Today's Little Leaguers — and there are millions of them each year — pick up on how to hit and throw and field just by watching the games on TV. By the time they're out of high school, the good ones are almost ready to play professional ball.

—Mickey Mantle
Yankees outfielder (1951–68)

Not a single player held out for a trade or a bigger contract. Nobody recruited anybody or induced them to play with new cars. Not even a tricycle.

—Edwin Pope
"What Do Children Know Anyway?" (1982)

I'll bet you don't know what is the first question Little Leaguers ask me. "How much money do you make?"

—Rocky Bridges
Reds infielder (1953–57)

Kids should practice autographing baseballs. This is a skill that's often overlooked in Little League.

—*Tug McGraw*
Phillies pitcher (1975–84)

Youngsters of Little League can survive undercoaching a lot better than overcoaching.

—*Willie Mays*
Giants outfielder (1951–72)

Generally in the Little League, you're up against a good pitcher who throws like hell. What does the coach say? Get a walk. Isn't that a beautiful way to learn to hit? For four years you stand up there looking for a walk.

—*Robin Roberts*
Phillies pitcher (1948–61)

Baseball is a kid's game that grownups only tend to screw up.

—*Bob Lemon*
Indians pitcher (1946–58)

Little League baseball is a very good thing because it keeps the parents off the streets.

—Yogi Berra
Yankees catcher (1946–63)

For the parent of a Little Leaguer, a baseball game is simply a nervous breakdown divided into innings.

—Earl Wilson (1907–87)
columnist

There is nothing better calculated than Base Ball to give a growing boy self-poise and self-reliance, confidence, inoffensive and entirely proper aggressiveness, general manliness. Base Ball is a man maker.

—A.G. Spalding
New York Times (1910)

When I was a kid, I used to ride my bike around in the winter, with my glove hooked onto the handlebars. There was always snow around, but I wanted to be ready, just in case one of my friends had a ball.

—Bob Buhl
Braves pitcher (1953–62)

So it really is just a game, huh? And if it's not being played for fun, why play at all? To learn values? That's asking a lot of a game. Play for fun and they'll learn the values, I think.

—Bill Geist
Little League Confidential *(1992)*

Only yesterday the fan was a kid of nine or ten bolting his breakfast on Saturday morning and hurtling from the house with a glove buttoned over his belt and a bat over his shoulder, rushing to the nearest vacant lot, perhaps the nearest alley, where the other guys were gathering, a place where it would always be spring.

—Douglass Wallopp
Baseball: An Informal History *(1969)*

My hitting was my ticket to acceptance. . . . I hit a single, a double, a triple and two home runs. My standing with the other boys, strangers just a few days before, was assured. The summer was mine.

—Richard Hugo
"The Anxious Fields of Play" *(1986)*

Baseball to me is still the national pastime because it is a summer game. I feel that almost all Americans are summer people, that summer is what they think of when they think of their childhood. I think it stirs up an incredible emotion within people.

—Steve Busby
Royals pitcher (1972–80)

The big league dreams of most youngsters are squashed by reality at a rather tender age. By the time they are fourteen or fifteen they come to know that their skills are simply too frail. They cannot hit the ball far enough, or throw it hard enough, or run with sufficient speed so they lay their dream to rest beside a trophy or two, or wrap it neatly in a varsity sweater.

—Stanley Cohen
The Man in the Crowd (1981)

When I was a small boy in Kansas, a friend of mine and I went fishing . . . I told him I wanted to be a real major league baseball player, a genuine professional like Honus Wagner. My friend said that he'd like to be President of the United States. Neither of us got our wish.

—Dwight D. Eisenhower (1890–1969)
34th President of the United States

A DOZEN GREAT BASEBALL NICKNAMES

"The Barber": Sal Maglie, Giants and Dodgers pitcher of the 1950s, who intimidated hitters by throwing inside pitches that almost "shaved" their faces. Shaving was something Maglie rarely did himself. During every start, Maglie sported a five o'clock shadow, which made him look as menacing as his brushbacks.

"Captain Hook": Sparky Anderson, Reds manager of the 1970s who seldom left a starting pitcher in a game past the sixth inning. Blessed with one of the deepest bullpens in baseball, the boss of Cincinnati's "Big Red Machine" wasn't bashful about lifting a starter at the first sign of trouble.

"The Crab": Johnny Evers, infielder with the Cubs and Braves in the early 1900s. Given this nickname for the way he attacked ground balls, Evers was later celebrated in one of the game's most famous poems. Franklin P. Adams's verse "Tinker to Evers to Chance" lauded the most famous double-play combination of the Dead-Ball Era, earning Evers baseball immortality.

"Dr. Strangeglove": fumble-fingered first baseman Dick Stuart of the Pirates, Red Sox and Phils in the 1960s. Stuart was one of the game's most feared sluggers, but his fielding was terrifying to watch. Once, during a game in Pittsburgh, Stuart speared a hot dog wrapper that had blown onto the field. Sarcastic Pirate fans gave him a standing ovation.

"El Goofy": Yankees pitcher Vernon "Lefty" Gomez, New York's most effective starter during the 1930s and '40s. His Hispanic ancestry and self-deprecating sense of humor earned him this sobriquet.

"The Hoover": Orioles third baseman Brooks Robinson, likely the greatest fielder ever to play his position. From the mid-1950s until the late '70s, Robinson virtually sucked up every ball that came his way.

"King Kong": Yankees outfielder Charlie Keller, a star of the late 1930s and early '40s. He gained the name for his mighty home run blasts, and for his hairy body and ape-like appearance.

"The Little General": Gene Mauch, manager of the Phillies, Expos, Twins and Angels. One of the most brilliant strategical minds in baseball history, Mauch never won a pennant in his two-plus decades of managing. He holds the dubious record of winning more big league games without a championship than any other manager in history.

"The Mad Hungarian": Al Hrabosky, Cardinals relief pitcher of the 1970s. Sporting a Fu-Manchu moustache and a fierce countenance, Hrabosky paced the mound, talking to himself before every pitch. Such bizarre behavior was tolerated during his heyday as the top fireman in baseball, but once his pitches lost their bite, his act grew comical, then tiresome.

"The Meal Ticket": Giants pitcher Carl Hubbell, the ace of the staff during the 1930s and '40s. A stopper of losing streaks and a perennial twenty-game winner, Hubbell kept New York in contention and always drew huge crowds on the days he pitched.

"Old Aches and Pains": White Sox shortstop Luke Appling of the 1930s and '40s. Appling never stopped complaining about the various ailments that bothered him, yet the more he bellyached, the better he hit. He batted over .300 in fifteen different seasons.

"The Toy Cannon": Jimmy Wynn, the Astros and Dodgers outfielder, weighed a mere 160 pounds, yet launched nearly 300 home runs during his major league career. In 1974 he led the Dodgers to the National League pennant.

THE GATHERING CROWD

The crowd makes the ballgame. How much pepper do you suppose a player would show if games were played to empty seats?

—Ty Cobb
Tigers outfielder (1905–26)

I'm waiting for the day we see the "wave" at the Metropolitan Opera.

—Al Michaels (b. 1944)
broadcaster

I have discovered, in twenty years of moving around the ballpark, that the knowledge of the game is usually in inverse proportion to the price of the seats.

—Bill Veeck (1914–86)
baseball executive

Why, certainly I'd like to have that fellow who hits a home run every time at bat, who strikes out every opposing batter when he's pitching.... any manager would want a guy like that playing for him. The only trouble is to get him to put down his cup of beer and come down out of the stands and do these things.

—*Danny Murtaugh*
Pirates manager (1957–64, '67, '70–71, '73–76)

All baseball fans can be divided into two groups: Those who come to batting practice and the others. Only those in the first category have much chance of amounting to anything.

—*Thomas Boswell*
Why Time Begins on Opening Day (1984)

One of the myths by which we live is that the "real" baseball fan loves a 1–0 game and "abhors" a sloppy 8–6 game. Even the most cursory studies show that fans love 8–6 games and are bored to death by classic 1–0 "pitcher's battles."

—*Bill Veeck (1914–86)*
baseball executive

All baseball fans are provincial. They don't want the best team to win. They want *their* team to win.

— *Art Hill*
I Don't Care if I Never Come Back *(1980)*

The guy with the biggest stomach will be the first to take off his shirt at a baseball game.

—*Glenn Dickey*
San Francisco Chronicle *(1981)*

It is a beer-drinker's game, a slow load standing at a bar and talking about unimportant matters. It is being at the park and coming back to the saloon.

—*Jimmy Cannon (1910–73)*
sportswriter

Baseball mainly attracts two demographic groups: boys under 14 and men over 60. Boys under 14 like it because their daddies make them play catch in the yard. Men over 60 like it because they have to piss a lot and they can do this while watching baseball on TV and not miss anything.

—*Dan Jenkins (b. 1929)*
sportswriter

Baseball is the most profane of sports, but even some of the mightiest cussers run a Sunday school second to urchins shunned in quest of autographs.

—*Edwin Pope*
"Autographs and Conscience" (1974)

The true fan is not only violently partisan, but very noisy. . . . I used to amuse myself with wondering what would happen if a group of fans of this order would turn up at a tennis match or a golf meet.

—*W.R. Burnett (1899–1982)*
author

Why would anyone invest in baseball cards? . . . These are not shares of IBM stock, certificates of deposit with guaranteed rates of return . . . why would anyone not sitting in the left-field bleachers through a hot August double-header think there is serious money to be made with them?

—*Paul M. Green and Donn Pearlman*
Making Money with Baseball Cards *(1989)*

They were beautiful and reassuring to behold, brand new and glistening crisply in their packages ... stuck behind glassed partitions and stacked on counters. An indication that the world was still in order, a promise of pleasant days and easeful nights.

—Brendan C. Boyd and Fred C. Harris
**The Great American Baseball Card Flipping,
Trading and Bubble-Gum Book** *(1973)*

There is a certain degree of truth that dealers like myself have "destroyed the hobby" .... critics have been saying this since the turn of the century. It's just not true. Baseball cards grew up, that's all.... What the old-timers won't accept is that this change is irrevocable. There's no going back to the days of casual trading. Cards are big business.

—Alan Rosen
Mr. Mint's Insider's Investment Guide *(1991)*

For many, baseball cards are the last toy as well as the first possession. You fall in love with them as a child, then leave them behind at puberty. They link the blue-water, lazy-day joy of childhood summers with the pride of blossoming maturity.

—Thomas Boswell
Washington Post *(1991)*

Today the rule seems to be not to touch your cards once you acquire them in order to keep them in mint condition, but back in the '50s, I couldn't go through a full summer's day without feverishly going through my card collection; letting my miserly hands run through the thousands of cards I kept in a box.

—Danny Peary
How to Buy, Trade and Invest in Baseball Cards *(1989)*

I wanted to be a big league baseball player so I could see my picture on a bubblegum card.

—Al Ferrara
Dodgers outfielder (1963–68)

I venture to say that there are millions of adults who would give almost anything to have been a major league ballplayer for just a day.

—Charlie Grimm
Cubs manager (1932–38, '44–49, '60)

The majority of American males put themselves to sleep by striking out the batting order of the New York Yankees.

—James Thurber (1894–1961)
author

A baseball game is twice as much fun if you're seeing it on company time.

—*William Feather*
The Business of Life *(1968)*

If you want to see a baseball game in the worst way — take your wife along.

—*Henny Youngman (b. 1906)*
comedian

I last attended a major league baseball game in Washington in the summer of 1934. It was the only one I ever got to; it wasn't very interesting, so I didn't go back.

—*John Kenneth Galbraith (b. 1908)*
economist

If people don't want to come to the ballpark, how are you gonna stop them?

—*Yogi Berra*
Yankees catcher (1947–63)

I do not hate baseball fans. Pity I feel, yes, but not hate. Quite the contrary, I believe the federal government should make every effort to see that baseball fans are accorded equal rights with the more fortunate among us. It's not their fault they got in with a bad crowd when they were young.

—*Andy Rooney*
"Real Men Don't Wear Knickers" (1986)

With those who don't give a damn about baseball, I can only sympathize. I do not resent them. I am even willing to concede that many of them are physically clean, good to their mothers and in favor of world peace. But while the game is on, I can't think of anything to say to them.

—*Art Hill*
I Don't Care if I Never Come Back *(1980)*

I sat in the reserved seats and felt uncomfortable. Everybody is so polite . . . in the bleachers, however, you can be vindictive. Nearly everybody else is.

—*Arnold Hano*
A Day in the Bleachers *(1955)*

The folks who "pay the freight" are the loyal fans in the stands.

I have played baseball when literally thousands of people were yelling at me. . . . I could yell as loud as any of them but not as loud as all of them put together. They had the floor, so I went about my business.

—*Johnny Evers*
Cubs infielder (1902–13)

I understand people who boo us. It's like going to a Broadway show. You pay for your tickets and expect to be entertained. When you're not, you have a right to complain.

—*Sparky Anderson*
Tigers manager (1979–   )

On the road, I liked to be booed. I really did. Because if they boo you on the road, it's either 'cause you're a sorehead or 'cause you're hurting them.

—*Paul Waner*
Pirates outfielder (1926–40)

Fans don't boo nobodies.

—*Reggie Jackson*
Yankees outfielder (1977–81)

The fans booed me . . . but I knew deep down, that they weren't booing me at all. They were booing their own disallowed wishes.

—Steve Fireovid
The 26th Man *(1991)*

The fans throw different things. Rock stars have nice stuff like flowers and underwear. We get batteries and knives.

—Bob Ojeda
Mets pitcher (1986–90)

Fans? All you have to do is smile at 'em and say hi and shake their hands. They're satisfied.

—Al Kaline
Tigers outfielder (1953–74)

I play for the poor man. I try to give a thrill to the lunch bucket fan . . . I know their plight. I worked in a factory in high school. The poor folk who lay out the hard bread to see a game. That's where my heart is . . . the rich don't need heroes.

—Leon Wagner
Indians outfielder (1964–68)

I've always been a firm believer that the game has never belonged to the owners. It has never belonged to the ballplayers. It belongs to that guy who puts his money up on the window and says, "How much does it cost to sit in the bleachers?" That is who owns baseball. And it has got to be kept that way.

—*Johnny Vander Meer*
Reds pitcher (1937–49)

I believe we owe something to the people who watch us. They work hard for their money. When we do not try one hundred per cent, we steal from them.

—*Roberto Clemente*
Pirates outfielder (1955–72)

There is always some kid who may be seeing me for the first or last time. I owe him my best.

—*Joe DiMaggio*
Yankees outfielder (1936–42, '46–51)

Time is of the essence. The crowd and players are the same age always, but the man in the crowd is older every season. Come on, play ball!

—Rolph Humphries (1894–1969)
"Polo Grounds" (1965)

THE OLD BALLPARK

I still remember walking into Tiger Stadium as a young boy for the first time and being amazed, first of all by the vastness of the ballpark and then the beautiful green grass . . . . the only way I can relate to that sensation now is the moment before the curtain rises in the dark theatre, waiting for the play to begin.

—Steve Boros
Athletics manager (1983–84)

I like to look down on a field of green and white, a summertime land of Oz, a place to dream. I've never been unhappy in a ballpark.

—Jim Murray
Los Angeles Times *(1986)*

I think a baseball field must be the most beautiful thing in the world. It's so honest and precise.

—Lowell Cohn
"The Temple of Baseball" (1981)

Ninety feet between the bases is the nearest thing to perfection that man has yet achieved.

—Red Smith (1905–82)
sportswriter

I had become as accustomed to an entirely new generation of ballparks, round as doughnuts, merry nursery rooms, and as artificial and indistinguished as the suburbs in which they nestled. They look, all of them, like gigantic tiered wedding cakes with their centers sucked out.

—Stanley Cohen
The Man in the Crowd *(1981)*

No two are alike. No two speak the same language. Each has a character of its own . . . . every ballpark reminds someone — a schoolboy playing hooky, an industrial giant on an extended lunch hour or a housewife with an escape from domestic drudgery — of a memorable event when a man and a moment met in unforgettable achievement.

—Lowell Reidenbaugh
Take Me Out to the Ballpark *(1983)*

While you're playing ball, you're insulated. All the ballparks and the big crowds have a certain mystique. You feel attached, permanently wedded to the sounds that ring out, to the fans chanting your name, even when there are only four or five thousand in the stands on a Wednesday afternoon.

—Mickey Mantle
Yankees outfielder (1951–68)

A ticket seller before a big ballgame is like St. Peter standing at the portals of paradise, holding in his hands the word on an applicant's fate. There *is* one pair of seats behind home plate? Heaven lies just past the turnstiles.

—John Thorn
The Game for All America *(1988)*

God love them — the familiar faces, the grizzled, toothless, cabbage-eared mugs of guys and gals who have been working the ballpark for years. Program sellers, ticket-takers, ushers, counter ladies, the whole crew. Not pretty, but as real as corn on the cob.

—Crabbe Evers
Murder in Wrigley Field *(1991)*

To a groundskeeper, the park is alive. The grass is his baby to be nursed, to be kept alive and beautiful. The soil is a soft cushion with feeling. The foul lines are the border to a beautiful centerpiece. The mound is a calculated summit suited to the great heights that can be reached there.

—Joe Garagiola
Baseball Is a Funny Game (1960)

[We're] a doctor, when the grass gets sick . . . a pharmacist, preparing chemicals . . . a dietician, prescribing the right food, adding minerals . . . we're weathermen — we've got to know when to water, when not to water.

—George Toma
Royals head groundskeeper (1969–)

Mother Nature brings a nice big rain and the grass comes right back, and no one pays attention because that's the way it's supposed to be. But you let something that's as green as this field go to hell, the whole world notices.

—Pat Santarone
Orioles head groundskeeper

A good groundskeeper can help you win a dozen games a year. He is the tenth man in the lineup.

—Lou Boudreau
Indians manager (1942–50)

When I think of a stadium, it's like a temple. It's religious. Artificial turf was a desecration. It violated the temple.

—Jim Lefebvre
Giants coach (1980–82)

Rugs belong on bald heads. They're bad for baseball.

—Keith Hernandez
Mets first baseman (1983–89)

I think it is better not to deny that artificial turf has made baseball faster, more aggressive, and more exciting . . . artificial turf has helped immensely to open up a game that had become slow and methodical.

—Bill James
Baseball Abstract *(1986)*

On artificial turf, the ball says, "catch me." On grass, it says, "Look out, sucker."

—Greg Pryor
White Sox infielder (1978–81)

If a horse can't eat it, I don't want to play on it.

—Dick Allen
White Sox first baseman (1972–74)

Could a hawker of peanuts and pennants as easily sell ice cream from a truck or refrigerator at Sears? Sure, and more profitably, too. But peanuts and pennants get him into the ballpark . . . . if life is, as Freud said, love and work, they have made baseball their life.

—John Thorn
The Game for All America *(1988)*

I've often wondered what goes into a hot dog. Now I know and I wish I didn't.

> *—William Zinsser*
> **The Lunacy Boom (1970)**

Baseball players are the weirdest of all. I think it's all that organ music.

> *—Peter Gent (b. 1942)*
> *author*

At a ballgame, as in a place of worship, no one is alone in the crowd.

> *—John Thorn*
> **The Game for All America (1988)**

I felt like I was part of something there, you know, like in church, except it was more real than any church, and I joined in the scorekeeping, hollering, the eating of hot dogs and drinking of Cokes and beer, and for a while I even had the idea that ball stadiums, and not European churches, were the real American holy places.

> *—Robert Coover (b. 1932)*
> *author*

Here is one place where caste is lost. Ragamuffins and velvet-breeched, white-collared boys stand in that equality which augurs well for the future of the stars and stripes. Dainty clothes are no bar to the game if their owner is not afraid to soil them.

—Zane Grey
"Inside Baseball" (1909)

Occasionally, like maybe once a season, they still play baseball on a weekday afternoon. This way, they don't have to throw the word "hooky" out of the dictionary and baseball can still call itself family entertainment. These always seem to be the most beautiful days of summer, maybe because they are so rare.

—Jane Leavy
Squeeze Play (1990)

As a nation we are dedicated to keeping physically fit — and parking as close to the stadium as possible.

—Bill Vaughn
Kansas City Star *(1981)*

It is interesting about people that leave early from ballgames. It's almost as if they come out to the ballgame to see if they can beat the traffic home.

—*Lon Simmons*
Athletics broadcaster (1981–   )

Crack of the batting-practice bats teams with soft organ music. In unison cheers arise and die back down. More hot dog, popcorn and peanut smells float up from below. The greatest gift, though, is to the eyes. Colors explode. Spattering the stands, people's clothes brighten in the sunlight. If the welcome is at night, the scene is even more powerful. Bright lights above shower the green field. It glows with excitement. Standing there alone, I always feel as if the stadium is embracing me.

—*Bob Wood*
Dodger Dogs to Fenway Franks *(1988)*

WHAT TO TAKE TO A GAME

Beside your friends, here are the essentials:

SUNGLASSES AND A HAT

It gets hot at the ballpark in July, and the afternoon glare can cut down your vision, so be sure to bring both along. Hats are tolerable during night games. (Team caps should *always* be worn, even when showering or attending important business meetings.) But sunglasses in the evening are an affectation that any true fan should avoid.

A PAIR OF SHARPENED NUMBER TWO PENCILS

Many fans like to score the game in their programs, so be prepared in the event a long rally wears down your pencil point. And there's always the danger of getting caught up in the excitement of the action, which could cause you to break the point in a scribbling frenzy. With two pencils, you're prepared.

A BAG OF PEANUTS

It's ridiculous (and often prohibited) to take your own beverages to the game, and even though ballpark food is overpriced, you're better off in the long run buying hot dogs, fries, burgers, and so on from the vendors. As author Art Rust writes, "Who wants to go to a party and bring their own food and drink? You're on holiday; you're not supposed to be encumbered with anything but pleasure." There is one exception to this mandate: peanuts. Peanuts and baseball are like milk and cookies, or surf and sand — an inseparable combination. But which would you rather munch — fresher, cheaper peanuts from your local grocer, or a puny bag of stale, expensive goobers that the concessionaires have had locked in storage since the Truman administration? No usher in baseball will confiscate a bag of peanuts you tote to the front gate. You'll spend less, have more to share with friends, and they'll taste better.

A GLOVE

Anyone age twelve or under is more than welcome to bring their mitt, in the unlikely event a foul ball comes their way. An adult with a glove at a game, however, is one of the most ludicrous sights in sports. Grownups are either supposed to catch fouls with their bare hands or have enough sense to bail out if the ball suddenly becomes a health hazard.

A NEWSPAPER

Remember, this is baseball, folks. Batters are fidgeting. Pitchers stare and then make endless throws to first. Relievers come in. Managers go out. Groundskeepers rake. Between the action, you'll have some time on your hands. So keep the crossword puzzle, book reviews, and stock quotations handy. But *never* take a book, especially one you value. First, it looks snobbish. Second, there is an unfailing law of the universe that any treasured copy of Tolstoy you foolishly bring to the park will invariably end up with a mustard stain.

BAT on BALL

They'll keep you in there gener'ly, as long as you can hit. If you can smack that ole apple, they'll send you out there if they've got to use glue to keep you from fallin' apart.

—Thomas Wolfe
You Can't Go Home Again *(1940)*

Hitting is the most important part of the game. It is where the big money is, where much of the status is, and the fan interest.

—Ted Williams
Red Sox outfielder *(1939–42, '46–60)*

Boston's Ted Williams, "The Splendid Splinter," was
the last man to bat .400 in a season.

Hitting a baseball is something that some people do better than others, and that a few people do very well, but no one knows why they can do it. Hitting a baseball is a mystery.

—Howard Senzel
Baseball and the Cold War (1977)

You can shake a dozen glove men out of a tree, but the bat separates the men from the boys.

—Dale Long
Pirates first baseman (1955–57)

For a ballplayer, the search for a batting stance is a kind of search for athletic identity. Is anything in sports so undeniably a signature as The Stance?

—Thomas Boswell
The Heart of the Order (1989)

Every great batter works on the theory that the pitcher is more afraid of him than he is of the pitcher.

—Ty Cobb
Tigers outfielder (1905–26)

The pitcher has got only a ball. I've got a bat. So the percentage in weapons is in my favor and I let the fellow with the ball do the fretting.

—*Henry Aaron*
Braves outfielder (1954–74)

Good hitters don't just go up and swing. They always have a plan. Call it an educated deduction. You visualize. You're like a good negotiator. You know what you have, you know what he has, then you try to *work it out.*

—*Dave Winfield*
Yankees outfielder (1981–90)

How can you think and hit at the same time?

—*Yogi Berra*
Yankees catcher (1947–63)

The art of hitting is the art of getting your pitch to hit.

—*Bobby Brown*
Yankees infielder (1946–54)

There is no greater pleasure in the world than walking up to the plate with men on base and knowing that you are feared.

—Ted Simmons
Cardinals catcher (1968–80)

There's only one way to become a hitter. Go up to the plate and get mad. Get mad at yourself and mad at the pitcher.

—Ted Williams
Red Sox outfielder (1939–42, '46–60)

You wait for a strike. Then you knock the shit out of it.

—Stan Musial
Cardinals outfielder (1941–44, '46–63)

I don't always swing at strikes. I swing at the ball when it looks big.

—Bill Skowron
Yankees first baseman (1954–62)

I'd rather hit than have sex.

—Reggie Jackson
Yankees outfielder (1977–81)

Hitters are like snowflakes. No two of 'em are alike.

—*Tony Torchia*
Red Sox coach (1985)

The good hitters hit the hanging curve, the bad hitters miss it . . . there's only about twenty or thirty hits a year difference between the bad hitter and the good one, you know. You hit those thirty hangers and you'll see your name up there in the papers.

—*Billy Williams*
Cubs outfielder (1959–74)

The most important thing is knowing why you made an out. If you know the pitcher got you out, you gotta clap your hands and say, "Great for the pitcher." If you got yourself out — by moving too quick, by trying to pull the ball, by coming out of your crouch . . . you should know that each time.

—*Rusty Staub*
Mets outfielder (1972–75, '81–85)

You'd be surprised how little many hitters know these days; they're as unfamiliar with the strike zone as they are with the sovereign countries of Africa.

—Tim McCarver
Oh Baby, I Love It! (1987)

There has always been a saying in baseball that you can't make a hitter. But I think you can *improve* a hitter. More than you can improve a fielder. More mistakes are made hitting than in any other part of the game.

—Ted Williams
Red Sox outfielder (1939–42, '46–60)

Carrots might be good for my eyes, but they won't straighten out the curve ball.

—Carl Furillo
Dodgers outfielder (1946–60)

When you're in a slump, it's almost as if you look out at the field and it's one big glove.

—Vance Law
Cubs infielder (1988–89)

We all have peaks and valleys in this game, but usually with the big, strong guys their peaks and their valleys are more severe. Slumps aren't going to be as deep or as prolonged with an average hitter as they are with the guys who do a little business with those cheap seats.

—Frank Howard
Senators outfielder (1965–71)

When you're hitting the ball, it comes at you looking like a grapefruit. When you're not, it looks like a black-eyed pea.

—George Scott
Brewers first baseman (1972–76)

When I'm not hitting, I don't hit nobody. But when I'm hitting, I hit anybody.

—Willie Mays
Giants outfielder (1951–72)

Most slumps are like the common cold. They last two weeks no matter what you do.

—Terry Kennedy
Padres catcher (1981–86)

I'm nothing for August.

—*Lee Maye*
Braves outfielder (1959–65)

To cure a batting slump, I took my bat to bed with me. I wanted to know my bat a little better.

—*Richie Ashburn*
Phillies outfielder (1948–59)

You dumb hitters. By the time you know what to do, you're too old to do it.

—*Ted Williams*
Red Sox outfielder (1939–42, '46–60)

How dumb can the hitters in this league get? I've been doing this for fifteen years! When they're batting with the count two balls and no strikes, or three and one, they're always looking for the fastball. And they never get it.

—*Eppa Rixey*
Reds pitcher (1921–33)

I was the worst hitter ever. I never even broke a bat until last year. That was backing out of the garage.

—*Lefty Gomez*
Yankees pitcher (1930–43)

How hard is hitting? You ever walk into a pitch-black room full of furniture that you've never been in before and try to walk through it without bumping into anything? Well, it's harder than that.

—*Ted Kluszewski*
Reds first baseman (1947–57)

You know, baseball is a matter of razor-sharp precision. It's not a game of inches, like you hear people say. It's a game of hundredths of inches. Anytime you have a bat only that big around, and a ball that small, travelling at such tremendous rates of speed, an inch is way too large a margin of error.

—*Rube Bressler*
Reds outfielder (1917–27)

Baseball is the only field of endeavor where a man can succeed three times out of ten and be considered a good performer.

—Ted Williams
Red Sox outfielder (1939–42, '46–60)

Nobody should hit .200. Anybody should hit .250.

—Charlie Lau
Royals batting coach (1971–74, '75–78)

They give you a round bat and they throw you a round ball. And they tell you to hit it square.

—Willie Stargell
Pirates first baseman (1962–82)

I'm a natural left-hander, but I bat and throw right-handed because that's the way I learned. But I eat left and drink left and write left. I'm amphibious.

—Dale Murphy
Braves outfielder (1976–90)

Man may penetrate the outer reaches of the universe, he may solve the very secret of eternity itself, but for me, the ultimate human experience is to witness the flawless execution of the hit-and-run.

—Branch Rickey
Dodgers general manager (1943–50)

Bunting is a very Canadian thing to do: obedient, modest, self-effacing. . . . As a baseball tactic, it practically screams out, "Excuse me." The home run is American; the bunt is Canadian, and when the bunter is done, he trots politely to the dugout, embarrassed by the applause.

—Alison Gordon
Sports Illustrated (1992)

Let's face it. Baseball has become a game of hit 'em where they are — where the fans are out in the 75 cent seats.

—Paul Richards
Orioles manager (1955–61)

The greatest thrill in the world is to end the game with a home run and watch everybody else walk off the field while you're running the bases on air.

—*Al Rosen*
Indians third baseman (1947–56)

I'd rather hit home runs. You don't have to run as hard.

—*Dave Kingman*
Mets first baseman (1975–77, '81–83)

It's my job to hit a home run. You don't have to shake my hand for doing my job.

—*Alex Johnson*
Angels outfielder (1970–71)

I don't know why people like the home run so much. A home run is over as soon as it starts. The triple is the most exciting play of the game. A triple is like meeting a woman who excites you, spending the evening talking and getting more excited, then taking her home. It drags on and on. You're never sure how it's going to turn out.

—*George Foster*
Reds outfielder (1971–81)

No one can stop a home run. No one can understand what it really is, unless you have felt it in your own hands and body . . . as the ball makes its high, long arc beyond the playing field, the diamond and the stands suddenly belong to one man. In that brief, brief time, you are free of all demands and complications.

—Sadaharu Oh
Tokyo Giants outfielder (1959–80)

GLOVE STORY

Defense is baseball's visible poetry and its invisible virtue.

—Thomas Boswell
Why Time Begins on Opening Day (1984)

Baseball puts you on the defensive. In the field, you don't know exactly where the ball will be hit, or when.... Readiness is half. Not knowing is what makes the game compelling.

—Geoffrey Young
"Second Base and Other Situations" (1985)

Let him hit it — you've got fielders behind you.

—Alexander Cartwright (1820–1892)
baseball pioneer

There's hardly a greater staple of the Hot Stove League than retelling stories of great catches in the outfield. . . . Bring three or four vintage baseball fans together on a winter's evening, the refrigerator filled with beer and nothing better on television than basketball, hockey or demolition derby, and chances are they will begin to regale one another with tales of acrobatic catches they have seen.

—William Curran
Mitts (1985)

They talk about hitting and pitching being contagious, but the most contagious part of baseball is defense.

—Mike Gallego
Athletics infielder (1985–91)

Of all the things we have in this game — hits and runs and stolen bases and home runs — the thing we have the most of is outs.

—Bill Rigney
Angels manager (1961–69)

The best player in a nine is he who makes the most good plays in a match, not the one who commits the fewest errors, and it is in the record of his good plays that we are to look for the most correct data for an estimate of his skill in the position he occupies.

—Henry Chadwick (1824–1908)
sportswriter

One of the unique aspects of the skill is that there is no way to verbalize it or teach someone else how to do it. Catching flies, it seems, must be completely self-taught at a non-verbal level.

—Peter Broncazio
Brooklyn College symposium (1983)

Catching a fly ball is a pleasure. But knowing what to do with it after you catch it is a business.

—Tommy Henrich
Yankees outfielder (1937–42, '46–50)

When I throw a ground ball, I expect it to be an out — maybe two.

—Warren Spahn
Braves pitcher (1942, '46–64)

No two ground balls are alike, so I take as many as possible. I'm a big believer in repetition: familiarity breeds comfortability.

—Walt Weiss
Athletics shortstop (1987–)

The key step for an infielder is the first one — to the left or right, but *before* the ball is hit.

—Earl Weaver
Weaver on Strategy (1984)

Most of the time, fielders must handle precisely those routine plays that everyone takes for granted. Therefore, one mistake, after nineteen perfectly executed plays, makes a man a villain. . . . In the sphere of ego satisfaction, the fielder has little to gain and a lot to lose.

—Leonard Koppett
The New Thinking Fan's Guide to Baseball (1991)

Our fielders have to catch a lot of balls — or at least deflect them to someone who can.

> —*Dan Quisenberry*
> *Royals pitcher (1979–88)*

What counts aren't the number of double plays, but the ones you should have had and missed.

> —*Whitey Herzog*
> *Cardinals manager (1980–90)*

Mistakes happen: if they don't, you're probably not playing aggressively enough. Fielding errors are like the bad-debt provision in a business balance sheet: you don't want a lot, but you get a little nervous if there aren't any.

> —*Tom House*
> **The Diamond Appraised** *(1989)*

If the out is there to be taken and you don't get it, that can make your ballclub droop. Then the mistakes multiply.

> —*Tony LaRussa*
> *Athletics manager (1986–)*

Do not alibi on bad hops. Anybody can field the good ones.

—Joe McCarthy
Yankees manager (1931–46)

Has anybody satisfactorily explained why the bad hop is always the last one?

—Hank Greenwald
Giants broadcaster (1979–86, '89–)

I don't like them fellas who drive in two runs and let in three.

—Casey Stengel
Yankees manager (1949–60)

There are some fielders who make the impossible catch look ordinary and some the ordinary catch look impossible.

—Joe McCarthy
Yankees manager (1931–46)

The first baseman is a big stiff, and since the beginning of time, big stiffs have played first base. He can't run, he can't field, he can't even bend over . . . that's because their real position is batter. . . . There is a formula for first basemen — the more homers they hit, the fewer balls they have to catch.

—*Pete Franklin*
You Could Argue But You'd Be Wrong *(1988)*

The middle infielders may handle between seventy and seventy-five per cent of a team's season total of chances, including most of the toughest assists. It's baseball's version of trench warfare.

—*William Curran*
Mitts *(1985)*

Good stockbrokers are a dime a dozen, but good shortstops are hard to find.

—*Charles O. Finley*
Athletics owner *(1960–81)*

You have to have extra-big ones to stand at third base, 85 feet from the batter when you're playing in on the grass, risking a whistling line-drive at your body or a one-hopper at 120 miles per hour that you have to dive into the dust to stab.

—Peter Golenbock
The Forever Boys (1991)

Next to the catcher, the third baseman has to be the dumbest guy out there. You can't have any brains to take all those shots all day.

—Dave Edler
Mariners third baseman (1980–83)

God watches over drunks and third basemen.

—Leo Durocher
Giants manager (1948–55)

Brooklyn's Jackie Robinson was a thief on the basepaths. He also robbed hitters with his glove.

Center field. On a baseball diamond, the most commanding and far-reaching assignment. It is an unwritten decree that when the centerfielder calls for the ball, all others cease pursuit. "He takes whatever he can get". . . . no other player has so imperative a mandate. He is a player whose boundaries are defined solely by his speed and his daring.

—Donald Honig
Mays, Mantle, Snider (1987)

What they call a baseball "glove" bears as much resemblance to a human hand as snowshoes bear to a man's feet. It's not a glove; it's a leather basket.

—Andy Rooney
"Real Men Don't Wear Knickers" (1986)

I don't care how big they make the gloves, you still have to catch the ball.

—Ethan Allen
Reds outfielder (1926–30)

I loved to make a great defensive play. I'd rather do that than hit a home run.

—Bill Dickey
Yankees catcher (1928–43, '46)

I got more of a thrill out of throwing out a runner than I did getting a base hit. I used to love it. I really gloated on it. . . . I still practiced all the time, even when I was in the big leagues. A lot of times, the other team would stop to watch me throw.

—Carl Furillo
Dodgers outfielder (1946–60)

A great catch is like watching girls go by — the last one you see is always the prettiest.

—Bob Gibson
Cardinals pitcher (1959–75)

In some games, there are no outstanding fielding plays. But when it happens, that's what I remember the longest. I may go home talking about a game-winning hit, but years later, when the actual game is forgotten, the super-fielding play will still be a sharp, clear picture in my mind.

—Art Hill
I Don't Care If I Never Come Back *(1980)*

CIRCLING THE BASES

Base stealing, the gentle art of sprinting and "hitting the dirt,"
is the finest drawn and most closely calculated play in Base
Ball, and the one that, above others, reveals the mathematical exactitude of the national game.

—*Hugh Fullerton*
"Hitting the Dirt" (1911)

It is the one aspect of the game completely free of luck. The
base runner who steals or takes an extra base on a hit and
run or an out has no bad bounce to contend with, no
infinitesimal physics of spin or ball-against-bat to deal with.
Only his mind, his skill, and his speed afoot are involved, and
those are constants.

—*Leonard Koppett*
The New Thinking Fan's Guide to Baseball *(1991)*

Thou shalt not steal. I mean defensively. On offense, indeed thou shall steal and thou must.

> *—Branch Rickey*
> *Dodgers general manager (1943–50)*

Having speed — and knowing what to do with it — are two different things. There are many who are swift of foot, but too slow of mind to use that speed effectively.

> *—H.A. Dorfman and Karl Kuehl*
> **The Mental Game of Baseball (1989)**

Baserunning is an art and a skill . . . if I'm on second, one ball on the batter, I'm going to try and get a big lead to distract the pitcher. My job is to help get ball two. Now the pitcher's got to throw a strike. Batter knows that. I know that. He's in a position to get good wood on the ball. He gets a single, I score. That's good baserunning.

> *—Dick Allen*
> **Crash (1989)**

If you aim to steal thirty to forty bases a year, you do it by surprising the other side. But if your goal is fifty to one hundred bases, the element of surprise doesn't matter. You go even though they know you're going to go. Then each steal becomes a contest, matching your skills against theirs.

—*Lou Brock*
Cardinals outfielder (1964–79)

A good base stealer should make the whole infield jumpy. Whether you steal or not, you're changing the rhythm of the game. If the pitcher is concerned about you, he isn't concentrating enough on the batter.

—*Joe Morgan*
Reds second baseman (1972–79)

The baseline belongs to the runner, and whenever I was running the bases, I always slid hard . . . I wanted infielders to have that instant's hesitation about coming across the bag at second or about standing in there awaiting a throw to make a tag. . . . there are only twenty-seven outs in a ballgame, and it was my job to save one for my team every time I possibly could.

—*Frank Robinson*
Orioles outfielder (1966–71)

Time and rhythm are baseball's moorings; speed can knock them both for a loop.

—Steve Fiffer
Speed, *1990*

When you're out on those basepaths, you've got to protect yourself. The basepaths belonged to me, the runner. The rules gave me the right. I always went into a bag full speed, feet first. I had sharp spikes on my shoes. If the baseman stood where he had no business to be and got hurt, that was his fault.

—Ty Cobb
Tigers outfielder (1905–26)

Stealing bases is like jumping out of a car that's going twenty miles per hour.

—Willie Wilson
Royals outfielder (1976–90)

Never trust a baserunner who's limping. Comes a base hit and you'll think he just got back from Lourdes.

—Joe Garagiola
Baseball Is a Funny Game *(1960)*

Sliding headfirst is the safest way to get to the next base, I think. And the fastest. You don't lose your momentum . . . and there's one more important reason I slide headfirst. It gets my picture in the paper.

—*Pete Rose*
Reds infielder (1963–78, '84–86)

In order to be an outstanding base-stealer, you have to eliminate the fear of failure. It's like being a safecracker. You can't be down there on your knees turning around every second to see if somebody's looking.

—*Maury Wills*
How to Steal a Pennant *(1976)*

I'll tell you with my lead that I'm going to steal second base. You know I'm going to, but there's nothing you can do to stop it.

—*Lou Brock*
Cardinals outfielder (1964–79)

If my uniform doesn't get dirty, I haven't done anything in the baseball game.

—Rickey Henderson
Athletics outfielder (1979–84, '89–)

You can be the fastest man in baseball but not be able to steal a base unless you can analyze the pitcher.

—Vince Coleman
Cardinals outfielder (1985–90)

I know if I can get the proper start, the greatest catcher who ever lived cannot prevent me from stealing second. All my attention is centered rather on the pitcher. He is the man I have to outwit and if I can do so, the catcher doesn't count in my calculations.

—Max Carey
Pirates outfielder (1910–26)

The best pitchers have the worst moves to first base, probably because they let so few runners get there.

—Tommy Harper
Red Sox outfielder (1972–74)

This is the key to base stealing, making the pitcher commit himself to home before you've committed yourself to run. Otherwise, once you're committed and he isn't, he can throw to first and you're dead.

—Dave Nelson
Rangers second baseman (1972–75)

Base stealing for me is another sport all by itself. It's a game within a game. I'm the mouse and the cats are trying to trap me.

—Maury Wills
Dodgers shortstop (1959–66, '69–72)

We are living in a very special time in the Live Ball era. This is the first time in baseball history that speed and power have flourished at the same time. . . . the modern base-stealer has a much higher success rate than in past eras — it is in the game's interest to protect that success rate and perhaps even to raise it.

—Craig R. Wright
The Diamond Appraised (1989)

I'm convinced that every boy, in his heart, would rather steal second base than an automobile.

—*Justice Tom Clark (1981)*

When we played softball, I'd steal second, then feel guilty and go back.

—*Woody Allen (b. 1935)*
actor, comedian, and film director

BIG-SCREEN BASEBALL

There are more films about baseball than about any other sport. Here are one fan's calls on the best and worst of them.

FIVE GREAT BASEBALL MOVIES

Pride of the Yankees (1942, directed by Sam Wood) set a high standard and introduced the narrative conventions that all subsequent sports film biographies would follow. The story of the "Iron Horse," Yankee first baseman Lou Gehrig, the film could have descended into maudlin pap as we watch the seemingly indestructible Lou painfully deteriorate from a fatal disease. Instead, actor Gary Cooper brings a quiet dignity to the role of Gehrig, who faces his death with humor and grace. The cast features many real-life Yankees, including Babe Ruth, playing himself in a vibrant and natural performance

It Happens Every Spring (1949, directed by Lloyd Bacon) may be the funniest baseball film ever made. A chemistry professor discovers a tonic that repels objects from wood and then uses the substance to become a star pitcher for the local St. Louis Cardinals. Oscar-winner Ray Milland plays the pixilated prof to comedic perfection, while the bizarre bounces of the doctored baseballs provide plenty of laughs in a film that could easily be labelled a live-action cartoon.

Damn Yankees (1958, directed by George Abbott and Stanley Donen) is an ideal marriage between two venerable American institutions: the national pastime and the Broadway musical. The story of a frustrated fan who sells his soul to the devil so that beloved Washington Senators can win the pennant is told with memorable songs, lavish production numbers, and breezy repartee. Even people who don't particularly like baseball can't help but be charmed by this high-energy fable.

Bang the Drum Slowly (1973, directed by John Hancock) is a classic "male weepie," the story of a backup catcher who discovers he is dying and the effect the news has on his teammates. In one of his first major roles, Robert DeNiro portrays the doomed ballplayer, a thick-headed cracker and bewildered lost soul who finally makes something of himself just as his life is about to be cut short. His once-aloof teammates rally around him as they race for the pennant, understanding at last the relative unimportance of the sport they play against the greater context of human relationships.

The Bad News Bears (1976, directed by Michael Ritchie) takes a probing view of Little League baseball that is both funny and insightful. Out of the mouths of a cast of angelic faces spews some of the foulest language of any baseball film in history, most of it hilarious. Sandwiched between the verbal and physical comedy are telling messages about the way Americans compete, the pressure to win measured against the feelings of individuals, and the fragile bonds between parents and their children.

FIVE ABSOLUTELY AWFUL BASEBALL MOVIES

Moonlight in Havana (1942, directed by Anthony Mann) tries to blend musical comedy and baseball with disastrous results. A singing ballplayer (Allan Jones) discovers he can croon only when he's sick with a cold. Yet those same sniffles and coughs also jeopardize his making the team during spring training. On this ludicrous plot device hangs the less-than-riveting outcome of a most forgettable film. Anthony Mann went on to become one of the great directors of Hollywood westerns, but you'd never know he had any talent after suffering through this picture, which stinks like a Havana cigar.

The Babe Ruth Story (1948, directed by Roy del Ruth) is likely the worst sports film biography ever made. Hollywood has often been known to take poetic license by mixing fact and legend in its screen bios. Here, the ridiculously sanitized Bambino becomes little more than a cartoon character. This is a sappy, juvenile, and totally unrealistic depiction of a sports legend who deserved a far better film. The real Babe was a street-smart, flamboyant showman. Those characteristics are missing in action in William Bendix's clownish portrayal. Instead, we're stuck with a none-too-bright Sultan of Swat, who abruptly leaves games in progress (while still in uniform), dashing off to hospitals to visit sick kids. Babe Ruth screened this film in the final cancer-plagued months of his life. Said one pressbox wag, "Seeing that lousy movie is what probably killed him."

Safe At Home! (1962, directed by Walter Doniger) attempted to cash in on the home-run headlines generated the season before by Yankee sluggers Roger Maris and Mickey Mantle. It relies on a premise that even its targeted small-fry audience could scarcely believe. A Florida youngster boasts to his friends that he knows Maris and Mantle personally and can get them to speak at his Little League banquet during spring training. Naturally, the kid has never met the M&M boys and must figure out a way to make good on his outlandish promise. Consider the fact that no one is ever even seen *playing* baseball during the movie, along with the wooden, awful acting of Maris and Mantle, and you've got a "comedy" where all the laughs are purely unintentional.

The Slugger's Wife (1985, directed by Hal Ashby) almost killed the baseball movie revival of the 1980s. In this profoundly unamusing Neil Simon comedy, an Atlanta Braves slugger (Michael O'Keefe) is closing in on a home run record, but can't hit unless his girlfriend (Rebecca DeMornay) is cheering for him at the ballpark. Yet *she* wants to further her career as a singer and isn't always available. So much for the plot. This picture tries hard to be both a fantasy and a real-life drama but succeeds at being neither. The contrived happy/sappy ending is the final insult to any true (movie or baseball) fan's intelligence.

Field of Dreams (1989, directed by Phil Alden Robinson) is one of the most beloved baseball films ever. It was a huge box office success, which makes its pompous posturing and disingenuousness all the more insufferable. An Iowa farmer (Kevin Costner) hears voices that instruct him to build a diamond in his corn field so that disgraced (and deceased) White Sox slugger Shoeless Joe Jackson can return to play. There's nothing wrong with suspension of disbelief here— indeed, the W.P. Kinsella novel on which the film is based is a certified gem. Unfortunately, this picture wheezes along using hackneyed, contrived plot devices that would be laughed out of any freshman scriptwriting class. More damage is done with long-winded and sanctimonious monologues about the majesty of "the game," and cardboard characters created strictly for the purpose of inducing easy tears from the audience. Bad baseball films are awful on lack of merit. But *Field of Dreams* is worse than most because it aspires to greatness, yet collapses under its own weight by relying on cynical and maudlin manipulation.

BATTERYMATES

Any baseball is beautiful. No other small package comes as close to the ideal in design and utility. It is a perfect object for a man's hand. Pick it up and it instantly suggests its purpose; it is meant to be thrown a considerable distance — thrown hard and with precision.

—Roger Angell
Five Seasons (1977)

Nobody likes to hear it, because it's dull. But the reason you win or lose is darn near always the same — pitching.

—Earl Weaver
Orioles manager (1968–82, '85–86)

Good pitching will always stop good hitting and vice-versa.

—*Bob Veale*
Pirates pitcher (1962–72)

I'm a pitching guy. It's the one commodity everybody needs and nobody ever has in excess. You *never* have too much pitching.

—*Frank Cashen*
Mets general manager (1980–91)

Connie Mack is believed to have been the first to say that pitching is eighty per cent of baseball. This is a bromide as familiar as the proposition that all brides are beautiful. The only difference is that unemotional statistics substantiate Mack, whereas a bride's pulchritude sometimes — to be chivalrous about this — exists only in the febrile imagination of the groom.

—*Stanley Frank*
"Pitching Is the Payoff" (1946)

The success of the hitter and the failure of the pitcher are not different things, but the same thing merely looked at from a different angle. So to say that baseball is eighty per cent pitching is, in a sense, like saying that the head of a coin is worth more than the tail.

—*Bill James*
Baseball Abstract (1986)

This being regarded as a Star Pitcher is a harder job than being a coal miner.

—*Ed Walsh*
White Sox pitcher (1904–16)

Nothing flatters me more than to have it assumed that I could write prose — unless it be to have it assumed that I once pitched a baseball with distinction.

—*Robert Frost (1874–1963)*
poet

If I ever find a pitcher who has heat, a good curve, and a slider, I might seriously consider marrying him — or at least proposing.

—*Sparky Anderson*
Tigers manager (1979–)

Pitching is just an illusion. You're dealing with a man's eyes. Make him think he's getting one thing and give him another and you've got him.

> *— Alvin Jackson*
> *Red Sox pitching coach (1977–79)*

A pitcher needs two pitches — one they're looking for and one to cross 'em up.

> *—Warren Spahn*
> *Braves pitcher (1942, '46–64)*

Pitching a game is really a memory test, like playing a game of cards where you must remember every card that has been played.

> *—Howard Ehmke*
> *Tigers pitcher (1916–22)*

Never the same pitch twice, never the same place twice, never the same speed twice.

> *—Ed Lopat*
> *Yankees pitcher (1948–55)*

When you go over a lineup before the game and decide how you are going to pitch the hitters, that is the way you must pitch them, because your defense is playing them that way. I have seen second basemen catch line drives . . . and outfielders catch balls that were ticketed for extra bases. Lucky pitcher? No, just pitching the way he said he would in the clubhouse.

—*Kirby Higbe*
The High Hard One (1967)

Is it a science to throw a baseball? No, it's mechanics. I don't know how much science plays in it . . . when you talk about the science of it — some guys can do it all wrong and still do it better than everybody else.

—*Norm Sherry*
Giants pitching coach (1986–91)

When you're a pitcher you're always doing analysis. You study the hitters. You remember what they hit, what they don't. You file it all away, and you approach each hitter with the knowledge you've stored. It gives you a sense of discipline, a sense of order.

—*Bob Purkey*
Reds pitcher (1958–64)

I benefitted from realizing that there was too much to think about, too many variables, too many distractions, if a pitcher tried to stay on top of every nuance of the game all the time. In my mind I narrowed my emphasis and priority to one thing and one thing only: the pitch.

—Orel Hershiser
Dodgers pitcher (1983–   )

The dumber a pitcher is, the better. When he gets smart and begins to experiment with a lot of different pitches, he's in trouble. All I ever had was a fast ball, a curve and a changeup. And I did pretty good.

—Dizzy Dean
Cardinals pitcher (1930–37)

I exploit the greed of all hitters.

—Lew Burdette
Braves pitcher (1951–63)

All they do is tell pitchers what not to throw hitters, but it's the defense that's the offense in baseball: the pitcher has the ball, and what the hitter does is predicated on what the pitcher does, not vice-versa.

—Roger Clemens
Red Sox pitcher (1984–   )

The Red Sox's flamethrower: Roger "Rocket Man" Clemens.

I always felt the pitcher had the advantage. It's like serving in tennis.

—Allie Reynolds
Yankees pitcher (1947–54)

A hitter doesn't know what you're throwing; he hits what he sees. If you can't hump it up there at ninety per, you've got to be deceptive.

—Tom House
The Diamond Appraised *(1989)*

. . . every batter has nightmares about catching a fastball between the eyes. Stare at him and plant that dream in his head. Make him afraid and he's half invisible already.

—John Sayles
Pride of the Bimbos *(1975)*

Pitching is really just an internal struggle between the pitcher and his stuff. If my curve ball is breaking and I'm throwing it where I want, the batter is irrelevant.

—Steve Stone
White Sox pitcher (1973–78)

What is life, after all, but a challenge? And what better challenge can there be than the one between the pitcher and the hitter?

—Warren Spahn
Braves pitcher (1942, '46–64)

Most tight pitchers' duels are quiet affairs, and the noise that occurs when a pitcher, especially the home-team pitcher, gets the last out in an inning while enemy runners languish on the basepaths is not a loud noise but rather a whooshing sound of relief.

—Arnold Hano
A Day in the Bleachers (1955)

I don't have Nolan Ryan's fastball, and I don't have Steve Carlton's slider or Mario Soto's changeup, but when I get to the mound the one thing I usually take with me is a good attitude.

—Rick Sutcliffe
Cubs pitcher (1984–91)

It's no fun throwing fastballs to guys who can't hit them. The real challenge is getting them out on stuff they can hit.

—Sam McDowell
Indians pitcher (1961–71)

Just take the ball and throw it where you want to. Throw strikes. Home plate don't move.

—Satchel Paige
Negro Leagues pitcher (1926–47, '55)

The first thing a pitcher has to learn is that he is not an island unto himself.

—Jim Bunning
Tigers pitcher (1955–63)

Pitchers are a different breed . . . they're looked at as more needy of emotional support than the regulars . . . the pitcher is the guy the manager jerks off the field; it's embarrassing. Even pitchers who are going good need support. Batters who are going good are fine.

—Larry Rothschild
Reds pitching coach (1990–   )

That's all you pitchers talk about — runs, runs, runs!

—Don Blasingame
Reds infielder (1961–63)

All pitchers are liars or crybabies.

—Yogi Berra
Yankees catcher (1947–63)

The pitcher is the happiest with his arm idle. He prefers to dawdle in the present, knowing that as soon as he gets on the mound and starts his windup, he delivers himself to the uncertainty of the future.

—*George Plimpton*
Out of My League *(1961)*

To a pitcher, a base hit is the perfect example of negative feedback.

—*Steve Hovley*
Royals outfielder (1972–73)

I throw the ball 92 miles an hour, but they hit it back just as hard.

—*Joaquin Andujar*
Cardinals pitcher (1981–85)

If I had a shortstop with a 25-foot wingspan, who could leap 25 feet in the air, all my problems would be solved.

—*Jerry Reuss*
Dodgers pitcher (1979–87)

If you can get an out on one pitch, take it. Let the strike-outs come on the outstanding pitches. Winning is the big thing. If you throw a lot of pitches, before you know it, your arm's gone.

—*Dwight Gooden*
Mets pitcher (1984–   )

A pitcher's life is one day of deliberate self-injury, followed by three days of healing, then a fresh injury.

—*Thomas Boswell*
The Heart of the Order (1989)

My arm still bothered me every time I pitched. I just decided Mother Nature was going to take care of her own, so I did nothing. I figured that God only put a certain number of pitches in my arm and when I used them up, it was over. But I always hoped I didn't use that last one up with the bases loaded.

—*Milt Pappas*
Cubs pitcher (1970–73)

A sore arm is like a headache or a toothache. It can make you feel bad, but if you just forget about it and do what you have to do, it will go away. If you really like to pitch and you want to pitch, that's what you'll do.

—Warren Spahn
Braves pitcher (1942, '46–64)

A pitcher with a damaged arm has about as much future as a bald Farrah Fawcett.

—Ron Luciano
Remembrance of Swings Past (1988)

The two most important things in life are good friends and a strong bullpen.

—Bob Lemon
Yankees manager (1978–79, '81–82)

Why pitch nine innings when you can get just as famous pitching two?

—Sparky Lyle
Yankees relief pitcher (1972–78)

The relief pitcher is the one man on a team who can make the manager look like a genius.

—Birdie Tebbetts
Reds manager (1954–58)

My shoes aren't so big that I can go out, and just because of who I am, get people out. I've got to have that killer instinct every time I take the field.

—Bill Caudill
Mariners relief pitcher (1982–83)

Pitching is the art of instilling fear.

—Sandy Koufax
Dodgers pitcher (1955–66)

It helps if the hitter thinks you're a little crazy.

—Nolan Ryan
Astros pitcher (1980–88)

I like to chew tobacco and see how dirty I can get the uniform. I spit all over myself. When I come into the game, batters say, "Hey, look at that hog with spit all over him. He can't get anybody out." That's what I want them to think.

—Charlie Kerfeld
Astros pitcher (1985–87, '90)

Some of these guys wear beards to make them look intimidating, but they don't look so tough when they have to deliver the ball. Their abilities and attitudes don't back up their beards.

—Don Drysdale
Once a Bum, Always a Dodger (1990)

I don't want to get to know the other guys too well. I might like them, and then I might not want to throw at them.

—Sal Maglie
Giants pitcher (1945, '50–55)

The beanball is one of the meanest things on earth, and no decent fellow would use it. The beanball pitcher is a potential murderer. If I were a batter and thought the pitcher really tried to bean me, I'd be inclined to wait for him outside the park with a baseball bat.

—Walter Johnson
Senators pitcher (1907–27)

Any pitcher who throws at a batter and deliberately tries to hit him is a communist.

—Alvin Dark
Giants infielder (1950–56)

I've never played with a pitcher who tried to hit a batter in the head. Most pitchers are like me. If I'm going to hit somebody, I'm gonna aim for the bigger parts.

—Bert Blyleven
Twins pitcher (1970–76, '85–88)

They talk about how dangerous throwing at hitters is. . . . I can think of more pitchers that have been seriously hurt by batted balls than I can of batters that have been hurt by pitched balls.

> —*Kirby Higbe*
> **The High Hard One** *(1967)*

I don't like losing a ballgame any more than a salesman likes losing a sale. I've got a right to knock down anybody holding a bat.

> —*Early Wynn*
> *Indians pitcher (1949–57, '63)*

Show me a guy who can't pitch inside and I'll show you a loser.

> —*Sandy Koufax*
> *Dodgers pitcher (1955–66)*

When I scout pitchers, I think of the line actor Tom Cruise's character was so fond of in the movie *Top Gun*: "I feel the need for speed."

> —*Syd Thrift*
> **The Game According to Syd** *(1990)*

The power pitcher — the man who can rear back and fog it by the hitter — is the brightest star in the pitching firmament. When he takes the mound, it is *showtime*.

—*John Thorn and John Holway*
The Pitcher (1987)

In the confrontation between batter and pitcher, it is the curve ball that makes the batter the underdog.

—*Martin Quigley*
The Crooked Pitch (1984)

A word about the slider: it is the pitch that has changed the game of baseball. . . . you can see the spin, but unless you anticipate it or the pitcher hangs it, there is not much chance of your hitting it solidly. It is a very tough pitch.

—*Lou Piniella*
Yankees manager (1986–88)

The spitter is a foul and unsanitary pitch. When some of the old spitball pitchers loaded the ball with saliva and slippery elm, it would be splattering all over the place. It can be seen from the stands, and the feminine clientele we have developed would find it objectionable.

—*Frank Lane*
White Sox general manager (1948–55)

It's high time something was done for the pitchers. They put up stands and take down fences to make more home runs and plague the pitchers. Let them revive the spitter and help the pitchers make a living.

—Casey Stengel
Yankees manager (1949–60)

I don't think legalizing the spitter would make much difference. They never stopped throwing it anyway.

—Pee Wee Reese
Dodgers shortstop (1940–42, '47–58)

Like some cult religion that barely survives, there has always been at least one but rarely more than five or six devotees throwing the knuckleball in the big leagues at the same time. . . . not only can't pitchers control it, hitters can't hit it, catchers can't catch it, umpires can't call it, coaches can't coach it, and most pitchers can't learn it. The perfect pitch.

—Ron Luciano
Remembrance of Swings Past *(1988)*

It's taken me twenty-seven years and I still don't know why the [knuckle]ball does what it does. If a man asks me how to throw it down and in, I say he's talking to the wrong man.

—*Hoyt Wilhelm*
White Sox pitcher (1963–68)

I never seem to feel as hostile toward the knuckleball when I listened to the French-speaking broadcasters in Montreal, who call it *le papillon,* the butterfly. You can't feel as bad about a passed ball knowing it was caused by *le papillon.* Striking out because you didn't hit *le papillon* makes you feel like you should get an award from some environmental group.

—*Joe Garagiola*
It's Anybody's Ballgame (1988)

I never worry about it [the knuckler]. I just take my three swings and go sit on the bench. I'm afraid if I even think about hitting it, I'll mess up my swing for life.

—*Dick Allen*
White Sox first baseman (1972–74)

There are two theories on hitting the knuckleball. Unfortunately, neither of them works.

—Charlie Lau
Royals batting coach (1971–74, '75–78)

The way to catch a knuckleball is to wait until it stops rolling and then pick it up.

—Bob Uecker
Phillies catcher (1966–67)

Catching is the most demanding day-to-day job in any sport . . . tactics pose him a continual mental challenge. He must consider the strengths, weaknesses and personalities of his pitcher and the enemy batters . . . he must wear equipment that is heavy and, in hot weather, double-heavy. He needs it, to protect himself against spike-shod runners who will try to knock him down and separate him from the ball, if not his intellect.

—Tim Cohane
Look (1963)

Catching is far more a learned skill than a raw talent . . . . You can't take the worst shortstop in the league and turn him into one of the best, but that may well be possible in the realm of catchers.

—Craig R. Wright
The Diamond Appraised *(1989)*

A catcher must want to catch. He must make up his mind that it isn't the terrible job it is painted, and that he isn't going to say every day, "Why, oh why with so many other positions in baseball did I take up this one?"

—Bill Dickey
Yankees catcher (1928–43, '46)

You have to have a catcher or you'll have all passed balls.

—Casey Stengel
Mets manager (1962–65)

The infield is like a steel net held in the hand of the catcher. He is the psychologist and historian of the staff — or else his signals will give the opposition hits.

—Jacques Barzun
"God's Country and Mine" (1954)

Catching is much like managing. Managers don't really win games, but they can lose plenty of them. The same way with catching. If you're doing a quality job, you should be almost anonymous.

—Bob Boone
Angels catcher (1982–88)

If you believe your catcher is intelligent and you know that he has considerable experience, it is a good thing to leave the game almost entirely in his hands.

—Bob Feller
Indians pitcher (1936–41, '45–56)

From the start, catching appealed to me as a chance to be in the thick of the game continuously. I never had to be lonely behind the plate where I could talk to the hitters. I also learned that by engaging them in conversation I could sometimes distract them.

—Roy Campanella
Dodgers catcher (1947–57)

A catcher is the wife of the battery couple. He must jolly [the pitcher] along to make him think he is the big cheese.

—Waite Hoyt
Yankees pitcher (1921–30)

Catchers are always trying to be an umpire's pal. They're usually two-faced brown-nosers who think that if they buddy up to you enough, maybe you'll cut them a break. Let me tell you something: Catchers will stab you in the back almost as fast as pitchers.

—Pam Postema, umpire
You've Got to Have Balls to Make It in This League *(1992)*

A catcher and his body are like the outlaw and his horse. He's got to ride that nag till it drops.

—Johnny Bench
Reds catcher (1967–83)

The wind always seems to blow against catchers when they are running.

—Joe Garagiola
Pirates catcher (1951–53)

Did you ever try to figure out why a catcher's batting average isn't usually as high as that of most other players? The answer: his hands are swollen and always in pain. Try swinging a bat when your hands hurt.

—Tim McCarver
Cardinals catcher (1959–69)

You'd be surprised how many catchers call for what they can't hit themselves.

—Keith Hernandez
Mets first baseman (1983–89)

There must be some reason why we're the only ones facing the other way.

—Jeff Torborg
Dodgers catcher (1964–70)

PLAYING TO WIN

There are only two places in this league. First place and no place.

—Tom Seaver
Mets pitcher (1967–77, '83)

Baseball can build you up to the sky one day and the next day you have to climb a stepladder to look up to a snake.

—Johnny Pesky
Red Sox infielder (1942, '46–52)

Close don't count in baseball. Close only counts in horseshoes and hand grenades.

—Frank Robinson
Reds outfielder (1956–65)

Somebody's gotta win and somebody's gotta lose — and I believe in letting the other guy lose.

—*Pete Rose*
Reds infielder (1963–78, '84–86)

There is no charity in baseball. I want to win the pennant every year.

—*Jacob Ruppert*
Yankees owner (1915–38)

Buy a steak for a player on another club after the game, but don't even speak to him on the field. Get out there and beat them to death.

—*Leo Durocher*
Dodgers manager (1939–46, '48)

The great American game should be an unrelenting war of nerves.

—*Ty Cobb*
Tigers outfielder (1905–26)

Ty Cobb of the Tigers was the fiercest competitor the game has ever known.

If you don't play to win, why keep score?

—Vernon Law
Pirates pitcher (1950–51, '54–67)

Baseball is a game, yes. It is also a business. But what it most truly is is disguised combat. For all its gentility, its almost leisurely pace, baseball is violence under wraps.

—Willie Mays
Giants outfielder (1951–72)

I've played a couple hundred games of ticktacktoe with my little daughter and she hasn't beaten me yet. I've always had to win. I've got to win.

—Bob Gibson
Cardinals pitcher (1959–75)

People say baseball players should go out and have fun. No way. To me, baseball is pressure. I always feel it. This is work. The fun is afterwards, when you shake hands.

—Dennis Eckersley
Athletics pitcher (1987–   )

If you've ever been around a group of actors, you've noticed, no doubt, that they can talk of nothing else under the sun but acting . . . it's exactly the same way with baseball players. Your heart must be in your work.

—Christy Mathewson
Giants pitcher (1900–16)

The only players that are having fun are those having a good year — feasting on pitching or blowing down hitters and garnering all the adulation that goes with it . . . but if you're not hitting or not throwing well, or are injured . . . you better look for fun someplace else.

—Dave Winfield
A Player's Life *(1988)*

Concentration is the ability to think about absolutely nothing when it is absolutely necessary.

—Ray Knight
Reds infielder (1974, '77–81)

When you make a bad pitch and the hitter puts it out of the park and you cost your team the game, it's a real test of your maturity to be able to stand in front of your locker fifteen minutes later and admit it to the world. How many people in other professions would be willing to have their job performances evaluated that way, in front of millions, every afternoon at five o'clock?

—Bob Feller
Indians pitcher (1936–41, '45–56)

One of the beautiful things about baseball is that every once in a while you come into a situation where you want to, and where you have to, reach down and prove something.

—Nolan Ryan
Throwing Heat *(1988)*

The best baseball people are Cartesians. That is, they apply Descartes' methods to their craft, breaking it down into bite-size components, mastering them and then building the craft up, bit by bit . . . master enough little problems and you will have few big problems.

—George Will
Men at Work *(1990)*

You got to play a hundred fifty games a year, so pick your spots. You can miss two games a month . . . so pick the days you're gonna be hurt, or you're gonna rest or you're gonna have a drink or two. The rest of the time, be on that field.

—Henry Aaron
Braves outfielder (1954–74)

There is a lot of luck involved in baseball. . . . And what is luck? Luck is really just a lot of practice, a lot of work. I think it goes back to bouncing the ball off the steps a jillion times and my God, pretty soon you have to get pretty good.

—Bobby Doerr
Red Sox infielder (1937–44, '46–51)

When we win, I'm so happy I eat a lot. When we lose, I'm so depressed, I eat a lot. When we're rained out, I'm so disappointed I eat a lot.

—Tommy Lasorda
Dodgers manager (1977–   )

When we lost I couldn't sleep at night. When we win I can't sleep at night. But when you win, you wake up feeling better.

—Joe Torre
Mets manager (1977–81)

I never slept when I lost. I'd see the sun come up without ever having closed my eyes. I'd see those base hits over and over and they'd drive me crazy.

—Robin Roberts
Phillies pitcher (1948–61)

It's tomorrow that counts. So you worry all the time. It never ends. Lord, baseball is a worrying thing.

—Stanley Coveleski
Indians pitcher (1916–24)

It's not my life, it's not my wife, so why worry?

—Willie Davis
Dodgers outfielder (1960–73)

Players seldom come to the realization that they are contributors to a losing cause. "Bad" teams are comprised of twenty-five "good" players, mostly looking for a way out. The losing is generally credited to the "team," an amorphous gathering, all of whom are blameless.

—Bob Hope
We Could've Finished Last Without You *(1991)*

Oh, hell, if you win twenty games they want you to do it every year.

—Billy Loes
Dodgers pitcher (1950–56)

Perhaps the truest axiom in baseball is that the toughest thing to do is repeat. The tendency to relax without even knowing it, the feeling being, "We did it last year, so we can do it again."

—Walter Alston
Dodgers manager (1954–76)

Everyone in baseball is so afraid of losing, but I've begun to think that for a team, learning to lose is a very important part of the game … you have to learn to *wait* in baseball, and losing tests that capacity.

—Roy Eisenhardt
Athletics owner (1981–87)

Every season has its peaks and valleys. What you have to try to do is eliminate the Grand Canyon.

—Andy Van Slyke
Pirates outfielder (1987–)

Losing streaks are funny. If you lose at the beginning, you got off to a bad start. If you lose in the middle of the season, you're in a slump. If you lose at the end, you're choking.

—Gene Mauch
Phillies manager (1960–68)

This losing streak is bad for the fans, no doubt, but look at it this way. We're making a lot of people happy in other cities.

—Ted Turner
Braves owner (1976–)

The only way to prove you're a good sport is to lose.

—Ernie Banks
Cubs infielder (1953–71)

How you play the game is for college ball. When you're playing for money, winning is the only thing that matters. Show me a good loser in professional sports, and I'll show you an idiot.

—Leo Durocher
Nice Guys Finish Last *(1975)*

If a tie is like kissing your sister, losing is like kissing your grandmother with her teeth out.

—George Brett
Royals infielder (1973–   )

It hurts a lot more to lose than it feels good to win.

—Bruce Hurst
Red Sox pitcher (1980–88)

There should be a new way to record standings in this league; one column for wins, one for losses and one for gifts.

—Gene Mauch
Phillies manager (1960–68)

Our phenoms ain't phenominating.

—*Lefty Phillips*
Angels manager (1969–71)

There'll be two buses leaving the hotel for the park tomorrow. The two o'clock bus will be for those of you who need a little extra work. The empty bus will leave at five o'clock.

—*Dave Bristol*
Brewers manager (1970–72)

After losing a game a player is required to file into the clubhouse as though he were a member of a silent order of monks. As long as he remains grave he is permitted to indulge in the buffet the clubhouse man has prepared.

—*Leonard Schecter*
"Baseball: Great American Myth" (1968)

I cannot get rid of the hurt from losing . . . but after the last out of every loss, I must accept that there'll be a tomorrow. In fact, it's more than there'll be a tomorrow: it's that I want there to be a tomorrow. That's the big difference. I want tomorrow to come.

—Sparky Anderson
Tigers manager (1979–   )

If you do everything right every day, you'll still lose forty per cent of your games — but you'll also end up in the World Series.

—Thomas Boswell
The Heart of the Order *(1989)*

A DOZEN BIZARRE BASEBALL INJURIES

While standing at the plate during a wild pitch, Atlanta Braves outfielder *Terry Harper* waved a teammate home from third. The Braves scored a run, but Harper dislocated his shoulder.

Oakland A's slugger *Dave Kingman* hurt his knee when he turned abruptly in the batter's box to argue a call by the home plate umpire. "Kong" missed eleven games.

Dodgers second baseman *Steve Sax* aggravated an old knee injury simply by letting a pitch go by. He didn't even swing.

When Sax made contact during a different at-bat, he connected for a home run. While completing his tour of the bases, Sax broke the thumb of third-base coach *Joe Amalfitano,* who was extending a congratulatory handshake.

Milwaukee Brewers outfielder *Gorman Thomas* was famished when he arrived at a restaurant. Anxious to begin his repast, Thomas bolted from his taxi cab, strained his back, and put himself on the disabled list.

In another costly dining mishap, San Diego Padres relief ace *Rich "Goose" Gossage* cut his finger while trying to crack a lobster claw during dinner.

New York Yankees outfielder *Henry Cotto* also earned time on the D.L. with a punctured eardrum. His was a self-inflicted wound—caused when he inserted a cotton swab to clear out unwanted wax.

Detroit Tigers designated hitter *Mike Laga* swung at and missed a pitch with such force that his bat came full circle and broke his wrist.

The Chicago Cubs had to scratch outfielder *Jose Cardenal* from their opening-day lineup when one of his eyelids stuck and wouldn't open.

In his most memorable starting assignment, Cleveland Indians pitcher *Bob Feller* brought his mother to her first-ever baseball game. In the second inning, an opposing batter fouled a Feller pitch into the stands. Out of the 45,000 people in attendance, the foul ball struck Feller's mom and knocked her unconscious. The ultimate irony: it was Mother's Day.

The White Sox bullpen became a danger zone when pitcher *Dennis Lamp* accidentally burned catcher *Marc Hill* on the face. Lamp inadvertently set Hill's beard on fire while lighting a cigarette.

Foul balls made Philadelphia Phillies outfielder *Richie Ashburn* most unpopular with a Shibe Park spectator. His first foul broke her nose. His second foul struck her moments later, while she was being removed from her seat on a stretcher. The victim was later discovered to be the wife of a local sportswriter.

THE MAN IN THE DUGOUT

Every player, in his secret heart, wants to manage someday.
Every fan, in the privacy of his mind, already does.

—Leonard Koppett
The Thinking Man's Guide to Baseball (1967)

Well, there are three things that the average man thinks he
can do better than anybody else. Build a fire, run a hotel
and manage a baseball team.

—Rocky Bridges (b. 1927)
longtime minor league manager

A fellow bossing a big league ballclub is busier than a one-
armed paperhanger with the flying hives.

—Ty Cobb
Tigers outfielder (1905–26)

It's like watching a man conduct an orchestra. All you see is him standing up there waving a baton. You don't see all those hours of rehearsal when he's working with the orchestra, trying to refine the music.

—*Eddie Sawyer*
Phillies manager (1948–52, '58–60)

For the most part, managing a team is a farce. One wearies of their studied idiosyncracies, the spitting of tobacco, the hitching of the belt, all the rest of the nonsense that goes with conducting a game that's juvenile enough to be totally understood by eight-year-olds in the Little Leagues.

—*Howard Cosell (b. 1920)*
broadcaster

I would like to be a manager for just one day. I'd tack a "y" on to the end of my name, chew tobacco and spit on the floor, sit around the office in my underwear and scream at the next five people I see. I feel better just thinking about it.

—*Scott Ostler*
Los Angeles Times *(1983)*

Bad ballplayers make good managers.

—*Earl Weaver*
Orioles manager (1968–82, '85–86)

Baseball has been good to me since I quit trying to play it.

—*Whitey Herzog*
Cardinals manager (1980–90)

I used to send myself up to pinch-hit whenever the wind was blowing out from home plate.

—*Joe Cronin*
Red Sox player/manager (1935–47)

There are surprisingly few real students of the game in baseball, partly because everybody, my 83-year-old mother included, thinks they learned all there was to know about it at puberty. Baseball is very beguiling that way.

—*Alvin Dark*
When in Doubt, Fire the Manager (1980)

Anybody who makes it out to be like a chess match between managers, well that's so much bullshit. It doesn't happen very often that you look that smart. My feeling is that when you're managing a baseball team, you have to pick the right people to play and then pray a lot.

—*Robin Roberts*
Phillies pitcher (1948–61)

I'll take all the criticism there is if we win the World Series. Criticism doesn't bother me. Only losing does.

—*Dick Williams*
Athletics manager (1971–73)

Catch them off guard. Get them looking for something, then hit them with something else. That's what baseball really is. The element of surprise. Always looking for an opportunity out there to create something. But get it quick. Right now. Not two innings from now.

—*Billy Martin*
Billyball (1987)

I don't believe in platooning your hitters. That's a lot of crap to me. If a guy can hit a left-hander, he can hit a right-hander. The pitch has got to come over the same plate. It's got to be a strike. Cobb used to say, "If you can hit, you can hit from either side."

—*Jimmie Dykes*
White Sox manager (1934–46)

Just hold them for a few innings, fellas. I'll think of something.

—Charlie Dressen
Dodgers manager (1951–53)

The toughest thing about managing is standing up for nine innings.

—Paul Owens
Phillies manager (1972, '83–84)

When I managed, I didn't like it when my players got hurt. If someone got hit in the wrist with a pitch, I'd run out, spit some of my tobacco juice on his wrist, and rub it in. It's amazing how many guys shook off their injuries once I started spitting on them.

—Jack McKeon
Padres manager (1988–90)

You do things my way or you meet me after the game.

—Frank Chance
Cubs manager (1905–12)

With my team I am an absolute czar.

—John McGraw
Giants manager (1902–32)

A manager should stay as far away as possible from his players. I don't know if I said ten words to Frank Robinson while he played for me.

—Earl Weaver
Orioles manager (1968–82, '85–86)

The manager is by himself. He can't mingle with his players. I enjoyed my players, but I couldn't socialize with them. So I spent a lot of time alone in my hotel room. Those four walls kind of close in on you.

—Al Lopez
White Sox manager (1958–69)

Managing is a lonely job. Players know you've got the whip and they steer clear.

—Bill Virdon
Pirates manager (1972–73)

The secret of managing is to keep the guys who hate you away from the guys who are undecided.

—Casey Stengel
Yankees manager (1949–60)

With championships in Cincinnati and Detroit, Sparky Anderson became the first manager to win the World Series in both leagues.

The true leader meets every man under him as an equal, then proves his right to leadership.

—*Hughie Jennings*
Tigers manager (1907–20)

I believe managing is like holding a dove in your hand. If you hold it too tightly, you kill it. But if you hold it too loosely, you lose it.

—*Tommy Lasorda*
Dodgers manager (1977–   )

I don't think a manager should be judged by whether he wins the pennant but by whether he gets the most out of the twenty-five men he's been given. The manager's real work, as I see it, is to reach the kid who's sitting over in the corner of the dugout and get him to play with the same attitude he had back in American Legion ball.

—*Chuck Tanner*
Pirates manager (1977–85)

I like my players to be married and in debt. That's the way to motivate them.

—*Ernie Banks (b. 1931)*
minor league manager

The manager's toughest job is not calling the right play with the bases full and the score tied in an extra inning game. It's telling a ballplayer that he's through, done, finished.

—*Jimmie Dykes*
White Sox manager (1934–46)

It used to be very prestigious, managing in the major leagues. That was when it was up to the player to make the manager like him. . . . The manager was the boss, a real authority figure. But all that has changed. Now it's the manager who has to make the players happy. He's the one who's always walking on thin ice.

—*Maury Wills*
Mariners manager (1980–81)

Individual grievances and pet peeves have got to go by the wayside. Generally, you don't have to worry about the guys who are playing every day. It's the guys who are sitting on the bench that are the ones that get needles in their pants.

—*Walter Alston*
Dodgers manager (1954–76)

You don't like your players or dislike them. There's no room for sentiment in baseball if you want to win.

—*Frankie Frisch*
Cardinals manager (1933–38)

They say I have to get to know my players. That arithmetic is bad. Isn't it simpler for twenty-five of them to get to know me?

—*Birdie Tebbetts*
Indians manager (1963–66)

The gruff old codger is history. "Communicate" is now the number one skill on my checklist for a manager.

—*Frank Cashen*
Mets general manager (1980–91)

Tell a ballplayer something a thousand times, then tell him again, because that might be the time he'll understand something.

—*Paul Richards*
Orioles manager (1955–61)

I had no trouble communicating. The players just didn't like what I had to say.

—Frank Robinson
Giants manager (1981–84)

Being a coach requires only showing up at the ballpark, hollering clichés and being able to play false sorrow when you lose.

—Jim Bouton
Ball Four *(1970)*

All coaches religiously carry fungo bats in the spring to ward off suggestions that they are not working.

—Jim Brosnan
The Long Season *(1960)*

Most coaches remain anonymous until they screw up. If a third base coach goes the entire season without being interviewed after a game, it means he had a perfect season.

—Jay Johnstone
Over the Edge *(1987)*

The manager of a team is like a stagecoach. He can't move unless he has the horses.

—Pete Rose
Reds manager (1984–89)

Gimme good hitting and long hitting and let the rest of them managers get just as smart as they want.

—Wilbert Robinson
Dodgers manager (1914–31)

When you play veterans, you may lose more games with them than if you had talented young kids coming up, but your chances of getting rehired improves drastically because you can never be second-guessed by the front office or blamed by the press. If you take what appears to be a gamble—and going with young kids is always a gamble—and you're wrong, you're gone.

—Dave Johnson
Mets manager (1984–90)

A manager wins games in December. He tries not to lose them in July. You win pennants in the off-season when you build your teams with trades and free agents.

—Earl Weaver
Orioles manager (1968–82, '85–86)

You don't save a pitcher for tomorrow. Tomorrow it may rain.

—Leo Durocher
Giants manager (1948–55)

For five innings, it's the pitcher's game. After that, it's mine.

—Fred Hutchinson
Reds manager (1959–64)

A manager uses a relief pitcher like a six-shooter. He fires until it's empty and then takes the gun and throws it at the villain.

—Dan Quisenberry
Royals relief pitcher (1979–88)

Managing can be more discouraging than playing, especially when you're losing, because when you're a player, there are at least individual goals you can shoot for. When you're a manager all the worries of the team become your worries.

—Al Lopez
White Sox manager (1958–69)

The way things are going for me, if I'd buy a pumpkin farm, they'd cancel Halloween.

—Billy Gardner
Twins manager (1981–85)

All managers are losers; they are the most expendable pieces of furniture on the face of the earth.

—Ted Williams
Senators manager (1969–72)

The worst thing is the day you realize you want to win more than the players do.

—Gene Mauch
Twins manager (1976–80)

If you're playing baseball and thinking about managing, you're crazy. You'd be better off thinking about being an owner.

—*Casey Stengel*
Yankees manager (1949–60)

Between owners and players, a manager today has become a wishbone.

—*John Curtis*
Giants pitcher (1977–79)

If a manager of mine ever said someone was indispensable, I'd fire him.

—*Charles O. Finley*
Athletics owner (1961–80)

I can think of three managers who weren't fired. John McGraw of the Giants, who was sick and resigned; Miller Huggins of the Yankees, who died on the job; and Connie Mack of the Athletics, who owned the club.

—*Red Smith*
New York Times *(1979)*

I don't think changing the President of the United States causes as much commotion as changing the manager of a big league ballclub.

—P.K. Wrigley
Cubs owner (1934–77)

Listen, if you start worrying about the people in the stands, before too long you're up in the stands with them.

—Tommy Lasorda
Dodgers manager (1977–   )

You never unpack your suitcases in this business.

—Preston Gomez
Padres manager (1969–72)

You never ask why you've been fired because if you do, they're liable to tell you.

—Jerry Coleman
Padres manager (1980)

The only way to make money as a manager is to win one place, get fired and hired somewhere else.

—Whitey Herzog
Cardinals manager (1980–90)

I think they recycle more managers than cans.

—Bill North
Athletics outfielder (1973–78)

Aren't all managers interim?

—Mike Flanagan
Orioles pitcher (1975–87, '91–92)

THE BOYS IN BLUE

Baseball fits America well because ... it expresses our longing for the rule of the law while licensing our resentment of law givers.

—A. Bartlett Giamatti (1938–89)
Commissioner of Baseball

Let's face it. Umpiring is not an easy or happy way to make a living. In the abuse they suffer, and the pay they get for it, you see an imbalance that can only be explained by their need to stay close to a game they can't resist.

—Bob Uecker
Catcher in the Wry (1982)

I couldn't see well enough to play when I was a boy, so they gave me a special job — they made me an umpire.

—Harry S Truman (1884–1972)
33rd President of the United States

Wanting to be an umpire is tantamount to wanting to be President of the United States. I can admire their fierce sense of responsibility, whether they are right or wrong, but sometimes it comes down to being a thankless job; however, the job must be done.

—Art Rust
Recollections of a Baseball Junkie *(1985)*

Umpires have the toughest job in baseball. Ever since the birth of the boos, they have suffered more abuse than a washroom wall.

—Ernie Harwell
Tuned to Baseball *(1985)*

I've been . . . hit with mudballs and whiskey bottles, and had everything from shoes to fruits and vegetables thrown at me. I've been hospitalized with a concussion and broken ribs. . . . I've probably experienced more violence than any other umpire who ever lived. But I've never been called a "homer."

—Joe Rue
American League umpire (1938–47)

Why is it they boo me when I call a foul ball correctly and they applaud the starting pitcher when he gets taken out of the ballgame?

—Jerry Neudecker
American League umpire (1965–85)

Many baseball fans look upon an umpire as a sort of necessary evil to the luxury of baseball, like the odor that follows an automobile.

—Christy Mathewson
Giants pitcher (1900–16)

My favorite umpire is a dead one.

—Johnny Evers
Cubs infielder (1902–13)

Umpires should be natural Republicans — dead to human feelings.

—George Will
Men at Work *(1990)*

If they did get a machine to replace us, you know what would happen to it? Why, the players would bust it to pieces every time it ruled against them. They'd clobber it with a bat.

—Harry Wendelstedt
National League umpire (1966–   )

They expect an umpire to be perfect on opening day and to improve as the season goes on.

—Nestor Chylak
American League umpire (1954–78)

It isn't enough for an umpire merely to know what he's doing. He has to *look* as though he knows what he's doing, too.

—Larry Goetz
National League umpire (1936–57)

The umpire must be quick-witted. He may not, like the wise old owl of the bench, look over his gold-rimmed eyeglasses, inform the assembled multitude that he will "take the matter under advisement," and then adjourn the court for a week or two to satisfy himself how he ought to decide. No, indeed. He must be "Johnny-on-the-spot," with a decision hot off the griddle, and he must stick to it, right or wrong — or be lost.

—A.G. Spalding
America's National Game *(1911)*

Gentlemen, he was out because I said he was out.

—Bill Klem
National League umpire (1905–41)

One of the really wrong theories about officiating is that a good official is one you never notice. The umpire who made that statement was probably a real poor official who tried to get his paycheck and hide behind his partners and stay out of trouble all his life. *Control* of the ballgame is the difference between umpires that shows up for the players and the managers.

—Bruce Froemming
National League umpire (1971–)

I think umpires have too much power, without any system of checks and balances. And the more money a player makes, the more the umpire tries to show off that power to him. Unfortunately, since I signed my contract, my strike zone has suddenly become a lot larger.

—Ozzie Smith
Cardinals shortstop (1982–)

Boys, I'm one of those umpires that misses 'em every once in a while. So if it's close, you'd better hit it.

—Cal Hubbard
American League umpire (1936–51, '54–62)

Any time I got those "bang-bang" plays at first base, I called 'em out. It made the game shorter.

—*Tom Gorman*
National League umpire (1951–76)

Umpire's heaven is a place where he works third base every game. Home is where the heartache is.

—*Ron Luciano*
American League umpire (1968–80)

I can truthfully say that I never did like umpiring. I stayed with it because I had to eat.

—*Lee Ballanfant*
National League umpire (1936–57)

The best thing about umpiring is seeing the best in baseball every day. . . . The cardinal rule of umpiring is to follow the ball wherever it goes. Well, if you watch the ball, you can't help seeing somebody make a great catch . . . see somebody strike out. That's what makes umpiring so much fun.

—*Henry "Shag" Crawford*
National League umpire (1956–75)

An umpire is a loner. The restraints of his trade impose problems not normally endured by players, coaches, management, press and others connected with organized baseball. He is a friend to none. More often he is considered an enemy by all around him—including the fans in the stands who threaten his life.

> —*Art Rosenbaum*
> **San Francisco Chronicle *(1965)***

The worst thing about umpiring is the loneliness. It's a killer. Every city is a strange city; you don't have a home. Ballplayers are home fifty per cent of the time, the umpires are not.

> —*Ernie Stewart*
> ***American League umpire (1941–45)***

It's not easy to be an umpire and a Negro, too. Maybe Sammy Davis would have a more difficult problem. He's Negro too, but he has only one eye.

> —*Emmett Ashford*
> ***first black big-league umpire (1966–70)***

Besieged umpire **Bill Campbell** gives **Boston Braves** manager **Casey Stengel** the old heave-ho in the tenth inning of a July 5, 1940 game against Brooklyn. Stengel's team lost—but not until the 20th inning.

When I first went into the American League, Johnny Rice told me that the toughest call an umpire has to make is not the half-swing; the toughest call is throwing a guy out of the game after you blew the hell out of the play.

> *—Bill Kinnamon*
> *American League umpire (1960–69)*

I've never questioned the integrity of an umpire. Their eyesight, yes.

> *—Leo Durocher*
> *Giants manager (1948–55)*

Despite all the nasty things I have said about umpires, I think they're one hundred per cent honest. But I can't for the life of me figure out how they arrive at some of their decisions.

> *—Jimmie Dykes*
> *Athletics manager (1951–53)*

Fans and players boo and abuse umpires, but there isn't one umpire in the history of baseball who has ever been proved guilty of being dishonest. I'm very proud to have been an umpire.

> *—George Pipgras*
> *American League umpire (1938–45)*

Umpires, you see, have one flashing button. They don't like to be shown up. Push that button and you're pushing the button on your own ejection seat.

—*Jay Johnstone*
Temporary Insanity (1985)

Umpires are most vigorous when defending their miscalls.

—*Jim Brosnan*
Reds pitcher (1959–63)

The job of arguing with the umpire belongs to the manager, because it won't hurt the team if he gets thrown out of the game.

—*Earl Weaver*
Orioles manager (1968–82, '85–86)

You argue with the umpire because there's nothing else you can do about it.

—*Leo Durocher*
Giants manager (1948–55)

BENDING THE RULES

The game of baseball is a clean, straight game, and it summons to its presence everybody who enjoys clean, straight athletics.

—William Howard Taft (1857–1930)
27th President of the United States

Everybody wants baseball to be kosher. They'll skin the sap who proves to them it ain't.

—Brendan Boyd
Blue Ruin (1991)

Crookery and cheating in business, politics, cards, and courtship, though rampant and profitable, disgrace those who get caught; but in professional baseball, seeking, finding and using an illegal edge is a prideful achievement.

—*Martin Quigley*
The Crooked Pitch *(1984)*

Cheating is as much a part of the game as scorecards and hot dogs.

—*Billy Martin*
Yankees manager (1975–79, '83, '85, '88)

The tradition of professional baseball always has been agreeably free of chivalry. The rule is, "Do anything you can get away with."

—*Heywood Broun (1888–1939)*
author

If a big-league player doesn't like cutting the corners or playing with "cheaters," then he's as much out of place as a missionary in Russia.

—*Rogers Hornsby*
Browns manager (1933–37)

I try not to break the rules but merely to test their elasticity.

—*Bill Veeck (1914–86)*
baseball executive

I'd trip my mother. I'll help her up, brush her off, tell her I'm sorry. But mother don't make it to third.

—*Leo Durocher*
Cardinals infielder (1933–37)

When I began playing the game, baseball was as gentlemanly as a kick in the crotch.

—*Ty Cobb*
Tigers outfielder (1905–26)

I owe my success to expansion pitching, a short right field fence and my hollow bats.

—*Norm Cash*
Tigers first baseman (1960–74)

We had better luck winning ballgames by stealing the other club's signs.

—*Kirby Higbe*
The High Hard One (1967)

I was the greatest hitter in the world when I knew what pitch was coming up.

—Hank Greenberg
Tigers first baseman (1930, '33–41, '45–46)

I corked my bats in the minor leagues . . . did it perfect, too. But I never corked in the big leagues. . . . What would happen if they suspended you? Damn, that'd be weak to miss the World Series because of corking.

—Len Dykstra
Phillies outfielder (1989–   )

A guy who cheats in a friendly game of cards is a cheater. A pro who throws a spitball to support his family is a competitor.

—George Bamberger
Brewers manager (1978–80, '85–86)

I never threw the spitter — well, maybe once or twice when I really needed to get a guy out really bad.

—Whitey Ford
Yankees pitcher (1950, '53–67)

My mother told me never to put my dirty fingers in my mouth.

> *—Don Drysdale*
> *Dodgers pitcher (1956–68)*

When a pitcher's throwing a spitball, don't worry, don't complain — just hit the dry side like I do.

> *—Stan Musial*
> *Cardinals outfielder (1941–44, '46–63)*

To me, drugs are like doctoring baseballs. I'd be too afraid I'd get caught. You never know who's waiting to turn you in.

> *—Phil Niekro*
> *Braves pitcher (1964–83, '87)*

I reckon I tried everything on the old apple but salt and pepper and chocolate sauce topping.

> *—Gaylord Perry*
> *Giants pitcher (1962–71)*

Hell, if K-Y jelly went off the market, the whole California Angels pitching staff would be out of baseball.

—Bill Lee
Red Sox pitcher (1969–78)

I don't put any foreign substances on the baseball. Everything I use is from the good old U.S.A.

—George Frazier
Yankees pitcher (1981–83)

It takes no talent whatsoever. You just throw it like a mediocre fastball. The scuff gives the break. . . . a good scuffballer can throw a ball a third as hard and make the ball move twice as much as an honest pitcher.

—Mike Flanagan
Orioles pitcher (1975–87, '91–92)

Someday I expect to see a pitcher walk to the mound with a utility belt on — file, chisel, screwdriver, glue . . . he'll throw a ball to the plate with bolts attached to it.

—Ray Miller
Orioles pitching coach (1978–85)

The general public will forgive them for cheating much more quickly than they will for losing. If they can't perform, there are a hundred guys dying to take their place. It's the perfect atmosphere to encourage breaking the rules.

—Dan Gutman
It Ain't Cheatin' If You Don't Get Caught *(1990)*

You figure they cheat at the ballpark, they'll cheat on the golf course, they'll cheat in business, and anything else in life. Players may laugh about it and say it's funny, but right down in their heart, they don't think it's funny at all, and they have no respect for a person who cheats.

—Bob Feller
Indians pitcher (1936–41, '45–56)

I've never had to cheat. I get 'em with what I got.

—Dave Winfield
Yankees outfielder (1981–90)

THE PRESS BOX

Baseball is the best sport for a writer to cover, because it's daily. It's ongoing. You have to fill the need, write the daily soap opera.

—Peter Gammons
Boston Globe *(1978)*

It is on the radio and in the newspapers every day, the only game you can follow on that basis, from whatever arm's length you choose. It is always there.

—Tom Seaver
Mets pitcher *(1967–77, '83)*

Anyone who thinks he can run baseball without a daily paper, can't run baseball.

—Walter O'Malley (1903–79)
Dodgers owner

Sports doesn't get covered like most news events. There is more opinion on the sports pages than anywhere else in the newspaper. I've never met a sportswriter who didn't have a strong opinion about something.

—Dave Johnson
Mets manager (1983–90)

Without publicity, baseball would be dead. And you'd be back on the farm, Roy, and heaven only knows where I'd be. . . . why do you suppose the ballclubs pay the expenses of those reporters in the training camps down south? Even take their families along, too. The publicity, Roy, that's what makes baseball.

—John R. Tunis
World Series *(1941)*

The papers knew more about baseball than anyone. It was the newspapers that compiled the charts and statistics that were the very substance of baseball history.

—Howard Senzel
Baseball and the Cold War *(1977)*

Sportswriter? The way the word is usually used, when introduced to strangers, it takes on the condescending sound of a rumpled, childish soul who goes to games for free . . . bitches about the high salaries of athletes, and stumbles through the week ill-dressed, ill-conditioned and hung over. Oscar Madison in *The Odd Couple* is a sportswriter.

—*George Vecsey*
A Year in the Sun *(1989)*

If I had my life to live all over again, I'd have ended up as a sportswriter.

—*Richard Nixon (b. 1913)*
37th President of the United States

For over thirty years I lived like a millionaire and was paid for it. . . . I travelled around the country, stayed at the best hotels, ate in the best restaurants, saw the best plays on Broadway, rubbed elbows with the rich and famous, mingled with the sports celebrities of the world and formed friendships that I'll cherish forever. I was a baseball writer.

—*Earl Lawson*
Cincinnati Seasons *(1987)*

I went four decades without tripping over a corpse or chasing ambulances. I was a sportswriter, a merry inventory clerk in journalism's toy department. Death for me came symbolically in the bottom of the ninth.

—*Crabbe Evers*
Bleeding Dodger Blue *(1991)*

I would argue that baseball would never have been considered the national pastime if the sport hadn't been so overcovered. . . . But I understood why this had happened. Sportswriters liked to get out of the house and on the road without their wives as much as ballplayers did.

—*Dan Jenkins*
You Gotta Play Hurt *(1991)*

Nothing on earth is more depressing than an old baseball writer.

—*Ring Lardner (1885–1933)*
writer

Ballplayers from the outback can be unduly disturbed the first time they see themselves misquoted or laughed at in a big newspaper. A team, like an administration, is as loveable as its press corps makes it.

—*Wilfrid Sheed*
Notes on the Country Game *(1981)*

What the hell do they need quotes for? They saw me play.

—*Tommy Harper*
Red Sox outfielder *(1972–74)*

To hell with newspapermen. You can buy them with a steak.

—*George Weiss*
Yankees general manager *(1932–60)*

If there's anything that bothers me about newspapers, it's the "unnamed source." When I read about an "unnamed source," I don't trust the writer. If you can't put your name by your comments, the comments aren't worth anything.

—Sparky Anderson
Tigers manager (1979–   )

Writers need the cooperation of the players for quotes and stories . . . players need writers for exposure and image-building. . . . So even though many players look at writers as obnoxious, overweight jock-sniffers, and most writers look at athletes as moronic, unbred, uncivilized threats to society, they all smile and do their jobs.

—Tom House
The Jock's Itch (1989)

A ballplayer has two reputations, one with the other players and one with the fans. The first is based on ability. The second the newspapers give him.

—Johnny Evers
Cubs infielder (1902–13)

Don't ever forget two things I'm going to tell you. One, don't believe everything that's written about you. Two, don't pick up too many checks.

—*Babe Ruth*
Yankees outfielder (1920–34)

Sportswriters expect you to cooperate with them just because they have the final say. They can write what they want, true or not, and you have no say in how the story reads in the paper the next day.

—*Dick Allen*
Phillies infielder (1963–69, '75–76)

I think most ballplayers read the sports pages, but I'm sorry to say that in most cases that's all they read.

—*Ted Simmons*
Cardinals catcher (1968–80)

Hell, if the game was half as complicated as some of these writers make it out it is, a lot of us boys from the farm would never have been able to make a living at it.

—*Bucky Walters*
Reds pitcher (1938–48)

Sometimes they write what I say and not what I mean.

—*Pedro Guerrero*
Dodgers outfielder (1978–88)

Everyone wants my time, and I don't have any time left. I'm a person, not a headline.

—*Vida Blue*
Athletics pitcher (1969–77)

They've invaded my privacy. I have no time for myself or my family. From now on, I'm not talking. From now on, I know I won't be misquoted.

—*Jack Morris*
Tigers pitcher (1977–90)

As a general rule, I acknowledge the wisdom of whoever first said, "Don't tangle with people who buy their ink by the barrel."

—*Keith Hernandez*
Mets first baseman (1983–89)

The only way to get along with newspapermen is to say something one minute and something different the next.

—*Hank Greenberg*
Tigers first baseman (1930, '33–41, '45–46)

I know what the word "media" means. It's plural for "mediocre."

—*Rocky Bridges*
Reds infielder (1953–57)

I can remember a reporter asking me for a quote, and I didn't know what a quote was. I thought it was some kind of soft drink.

—*Joe DiMaggio*
Yankees outfielder (1936–41, '46–51)

The marriage of Joe DiMaggio and Marilyn Monroe—a
pairing made in headline heaven—lasted all of 274 days.

Pour hot water over a sportswriter and you'll get instant shit.

—Ted Williams
Red Sox outfielder (1939–42, '46–60)

There are 300,000 sportswriters and they're all against me. Every one.

—Joaquin Andujar
Cardinals pitcher (1981–85)

I never read the papers. It isn't healthy for professional athletes.

—R.J. Reynolds
Pirates outfielder (1985–90)

The Lord taught me to love everybody, but the last ones I learned to love were the sportswriters.

—Alvin Dark
Indians manager (1968–71)

Thirty-five years ago I was talking to a reporter in New York. The next day, I picked up his newspaper in the hotel. I read his story. It wasn't like anything I had said. And I haven't read a newspaper since.

—*Al Smith*
Indians infielder (1953–57)

Some ballplayers think the writers are always out to knock them. That's silly. Four-fifths of them will write what's good about you if they can.

—*Casey Stengel*
Yankees manager (1949–60)

If players could only understand that credibility is all. My making justifiable criticism when it's called for validates the praise I'm more than willing to heap on them when they deserve it.

—*Tim McCarver*
Oh Baby, I Love It! *(1987)*

I'm going to Radio Shack to buy one of those headsets like the broadcasters use. It seems as soon as you put them on, you get one hundred times smarter. ·

—Nick Leyva
Phillies manager (1989–91)

I like radio better than television because if you make a mistake on radio, they don't know. You can make up anything on the radio.

—Phil Rizzuto (b. 1917)
Yankees broadcaster

The announcer is an extension of the team's public relations department. . . . If it's raining, he tells you not to fear, because the weather will clear. In fact, this rain delay is a blessing in disguise because it gives you more time to get down to the ballpark and buy tickets and hot dogs.

—Pete Franklin
You Could Argue But You'd Be Wrong *(1988)*

Baseball is the only game you can see on the radio.

—Phil Hersh
Chicago Tribune *(1985)*

Broadcasting is a lot of fun, but it's not like baseball. You don't control your own destiny. Ballplayers in the TV booth are like streetcars, you come and go.

—Jim "Mudcat" Grant
Indians broadcaster (1974–79)

FIVE BOOKS THAT CHANGED

BASEBALL WRITING

BERNARD MALAMUD'S <u>THE NATURAL</u> (1952)

Before *The Natural,* virtually all of baseball fiction was written for younger audiences. Authors such as John R. Tunis and Claire Bee penned inspiring tales of young, clean-living athletes who usually ripped the clutch hit when the sacks were full in the bottom of the ninth. Malamud broke literary ground by creating a baseball world devoid of such familiarities. *The Natural* is mythic in narrative, nihilistic in tone. The hero, Roy Hobbs, is an athletically gifted but flawed man with a weakness for fallen women and the gambler's dollar.

Drawing from Arthurian legend as well as the true-life

incidents of the 1919 Black Sox scandal and the 1949 shooting of big-leaguer Eddie Waitkus, Malamud weaves the rags-to-riches story of a ballplayer who nearly leads a last-place team to a pennant. The uplifting climax of the 1984 film version with Robert Redford bears no resemblance to the downbeat finale of Malamud's original. The novel, while frequently humorous, is ultimately a portrait of the darker side of a sport that previously had been depicted as wholesome and virtuous.

CHARLES EINSTEIN'S
THE FIRESIDE BOOK OF BASEBALL (1956)

The Fireside Book of Baseball systematically gathered more great writing and artwork on the national pastime than any anthology previously published. Editor Einstein poured through a half-century of novels, newspaper articles, magazine pieces, and illustration sources to produce a collection that still serves as a model for its genre more than thirty years later.

More than one hundred selections are included, all by different authors. They range from on-the-spot reportage to fiction, poetry to cartoons. Pieces by such literary legends as Paul Gallico, James Thurber, and Thomas Wolfe appear alongside eyewitness accounts of newspaper columnists and beat reporters. Eloquent portraits of baseball icons Connie Mack, Dizzy Dean, and Branch Rickey are also included.

So popular was this collection that two volumes of additional writing were released in 1958 and 1968 — both carefully overseen by Einstein. Any sports anthology (baseball and otherwise) since published has shamelessly — and correctly — attempted to copy *Fireside*'s flowing format of prose, poetry, and pictures.

LAWRENCE RITTER'S
THE GLORY OF THEIR TIMES (1966)

Library shelves today are fairly groaning from the weight of baseball oral histories. Many an author and publisher have effortlessly enriched their coffers by sticking microphones in the faces of retired ballplayers, then transcribing their remembrances to the printed page. Lawrence Ritter did it first — and still best — with *The Glory of Their Times.*

Ritter seemed an unlikely pioneer of baseball oral history. He was a professor of finance at New York University, not a sportswriter. Yet it seemed to him that many rich anecdotes and recollections would accompany aging ballplayers to their graves unless someone recorded and then published them. Ritter set out to speak with as many early-day stars as he could. He not only found them but also asked the right questions, proving his knowledgeable depth of baseball scholarship.

Ritter's (and our) reward was a treasury of surprisingly candid and insightful responses from such players as Sam Crawford, Edd Roush, Chief Meyers, Lefty O'Doul, and Goose Goslin — twenty-six individuals in all. Ritter then refined their responses into a seamless flow of first-person recollections, resulting in the most vivid depiction of early twentieth-century baseball in existence.

JOSEPH REICHLER'S
THE BASEBALL ENCYCLOPEDIA (1969)

When sportswriter-turned-league executive Reichler released the first edition of *The Baseball Encyclopedia* during professional baseball's centennial season, he revealed a world of statistical data never before seen in one volume. Prior to its publication, historians and fans had had no single source to turn to in their search for answers.

Here, finally, was a source with year-by-year stats for every player who ever suited up in the big leagues. Also included were seasonal statistics for every ballclub, tables of lifetime leaders in all major categories, and World Series and All-Star Game results. In subsequent editions, award-winners, trades, and Negro Leagues data were added. The research and statistical wave that permeates baseball today was born in the pages of Reichler's massive volume.

It has spawned a number of imitators, including *The Sports Encyclopedia: Baseball* and *Total Baseball*, both excellent sources with additional data not included in the original *Encyclopedia*. But "Big Mac" (the *Encyclopedia*'s nickname, since it is published by Macmillan) is still universally acknowledged as the most indispensable book in any baseball library.

JIM BOUTON AND LEONARD SCHECTER'S BALL FOUR (1970)

In 1969, Seattle Pilots relief pitcher Jim Bouton decided to keep a daily diary of the baseball season, then write a book about baseball from the inside. Others had done this before (notably Reds pitcher Jim Brosnan's *The Long Season* in 1960), but no one wrote more graphically or punctured more myths about the national pastime than Bouton did in this seminal shocker.

In *Ball Four*, fans learn of drug abuse, drunkenness, extramarital sex, voyeurism, and childish pranks, as well as incidents that shatter the simon-pure images of some of the game's most famous players. In shocking, often hilarious detail, Bouton reveals the stifling conformity that grips players and management, painting an unflattering portrait of the modern big leaguer.

Not surprisingly, the book made Bouton unwelcome in virtually all baseball circles. It also ushered in a new era in baseball book publishing. Sanitized recitations of names and dates were no longer enough to sell a story. Ironically, it was Bouton's love for the very purity of the national pastime that caused him to criticize those who would destroy it. This man, perceived as an enemy of baseball, probably loved the sport as much as anyone who ever played the game.

YOU CAN LOOK IT UP

And so, finally, he found his way back to baseball. Nothing like it, really. Not the actual game so much — to tell the truth, real baseball bored him — but rather the records, the statistics. . . . And no other activity in the world had so precise and comprehensive a history, so specific an epic, and at the same time, strange as it seemed, so much ultimate mystery.

—Robert Coover
The Universal Baseball Association (1968)

Baseball fans love numbers. They love to swirl them around their mouths like Bourdeaux wine.

—Pat Conroy (b. 1945)
author

A baseball fan has the digestive apparatus of a billy goat. He can, and does, devour any set of diamond statistics with an insatiable appetite and then nuzzles hungrily for more.

—Arthur Daley (1904–74)
sportswriter

I began soaking up records like a sea sponge before I even knew what they meant. I like the way you could read around baseball without ever getting to the game at all.

—Wilfrid Sheed (b. 1930)
author

I don't pay any attention to statistics on the stock market, the weather, the crime rate, the gross national product, the circulation of magazines, the ebb and flow of literacy among football fans: just baseball. . . . Baseball statistics, unlike the statistics in any other area, have acquired the powers of language.

—Bill James
Baseball Abstract (1985)

I don't care what or who, a record is a record. A triumph. Something to be cherished.

—Seymour Siwoff (b. 1925)
Elias Sports Bureau

The record of an event has the power to re-create that event. Statistics is the key to metaphor ... there is nothing that can compare with the excitement of assigning a precise and mathematical value to a central mystery of life.

—*Howard Senzel*
Baseball and the Cold War (1977)

The box score is the catechism of baseball, ready to surrender its truth to the knowing eye.

—*Stanley Cohen*
The Man in the Crowd (1981)

In most lines of work, there is no record. The good things you do often go unnoticed or are quickly forgotten, and the mistakes you make go mostly the same way. Baseball is only a game, but they keep a book on you. . . . When it's all over for you, the game has got you measured.

—*Joe Garagiola*
Baseball Is a Funny Game (1960)

Baseball is a game of statistics, and I feel that records are made to be broken. I'm just stubborn enough to want to break records just to prove that we modern-day ballplayers can do something better than the old-timers.

—*Maury Wills*
Dodgers shortstop (1959–66, '69–72)

There have always been players who, without compiling impressive figures, had a flair for doing the right thing at the crucial moment, and they have usually been popular and comparatively well-paid. But the guys who come in demanding million dollar deals, if they want to be taken seriously, had better have big numbers in the proper columns after their names.

—*Art Hill*
I Don't Care if I Never Come Back *(1980)*

There is no major league record held by a rookie. It's revealing to see just how far the rookie marks are below the single season marks. This is a testament to how difficult the game is to learn and to play.

—*Luke Salisbury*
The Answer Is Baseball *(1989)*

The problem that some of us had was that . . . the data is simply that — data, with no real practical purpose. There was a feeling that the players were being judged only from the eyes of computers, and no matter what any rotisserian says, you do have to *watch* Barry Larkin or Alan Trammell to appreciate just how wonderful each is.

—Peter Gammons
Baseball Scoreboard (1991)

Statistics are overrated. Championships are won in the clubhouse.

—Andy Messersmith
Angels pitcher (1968–72)

Statistics are used by baseball fans in much the same way that a drunk leans against a street lamp; it's there more for support than enlightenment.

—Vin Scully (b. 1927)
Dodgers broadcaster

I never keep a scorecard or the batting averages. I hate statistics. What I got to know I keep in my head.

—Dizzy Dean (1911–74)
broadcaster

Statistics are like a girl in a fine bikini. It shows a lot, but it doesn't show everything.

—*Toby Harrah*
Rangers infielder (1972–78, '85–86)

Statistics are about as interesting as first base coaches.

—*Jim Bouton*
Yankees pitcher (1962–68)

They can make two hundred-fifty bats out of one good tree. How's that for a statistic, baseball fans?

—*Andy Rooney*
"60 Minutes" (1981)

If you're tired of statistics used as "filler" material in newspapers and magazines . . . that's part of the price we pay for living in a free society. It's an annoyance, but look at it this way: if, after two hundred years of the Constitution, we still can't keep guns out of the hands of the wrong people, how can we expect to do that with baseball statistics?

—*Steve Hirdt*
Elias Baseball Analyst *(1989)*

Baseball may be loved without statistics, but it cannot be understood without them. Statistics are what makes baseball a sport rather than a spectacle, what makes its past as worthy of our interest as well as its present.

—John Thorn and Pete Palmer
The Hidden Game of Baseball *(1984)*

World War III would render all baseball statistics meaning-less.

—John Lowenstein
Orioles outfielder (1979–85)

FIFTY AMAZING REAL NAMES OF MAJOR-LEAGUE PLAYERS

Porfirio Altamirano
Maurice Archdeacon
Cuno Barragan
Matt Batts
Reno Bertoia
Del Bissonette
Ossie Bluege
Frenchy Bordagaray
Putsy Caballero
Estel Crabtree
Gavvy Cravath
Kiki Cuyler
Whammy Douglas

Taylor Douthit
Darcy Fast
Boo Ferriss
Cesar Geronimo
Carden Gillenwater
Guido Grilli
Atlee Hammaker
Drungo Hazewood
Gomer Hodge
Dane Iorg
Sig Jakucki
Elmer Klumpp
Clyde Kluttz

Coco Laboy
Lerrin LaGrow
Greg Legg
Candy Maldonado
Van Lingle Mungo
Rowland Office
Laurin Pepper
Biff Pocoroba
Rolando Roomes
Butch Rounsaville
Slim Sallee
Chico Salmon

Razor Shines
Urban Shocker
Costen Shockley
Sibby Sisti
Jigger Statz
Faye Throneberry
Dizzy Trout
Vito Valentinetti
Coot Veal
Burgess Whitehead
Dooley Womack
Dom Zanni

CLYDE KLUTTZ

Clyde Kluttz made a bigger name for himself as a Yankee scout than as a player.

219

THE BUSINESS OF BASEBALL

Baseball is too much of a sport to be a business and too much of a business to be a sport.

—P.K. Wrigley
Cubs owner (1932–77)

It's a business. If I could be making more money down in the zinc mines, I'd be mining zinc.

—Roger Maris
Yankees outfielder (1960–66)

Baseball isn't a business, it's more like a disease.

—Walter O'Malley (1903–79)
Dodgers owner

I'm going to write a book, *How to Make a Small Fortune in Baseball* — you start with a large fortune.

—Ruly Carpenter
Phillies owner (1973–81)

What you've got to have in baseball is pitching, speed and money.

—Ted Turner
Braves owner (1976–)

We live by the Golden Rule. Those who have the gold make the rules.

—Buzzie Bavasi
Dodgers general manager (1951–68)

There was a time when the National League stood for integrity and fair dealing; today it stands for dollars and cents.

—John Montgomery Ward
Giants shortstop (1883–89)

What has happened is that all your life you operated businesses in such a way that you could one day afford to buy a baseball team. And then you buy the team and forget all the business practices that enabled you to buy it.

—George Steinbrenner
Yankees owner (1973–90, '93–   )

Today you build the club for the immediate season, not the long-range future. What's that they say? The future is now.

—Hank Peters
Orioles general manager (1976–87)

When the great scorer comes to mark against your name, it's not whether you won or lost but how many paid to see the game.

—Peter Bavasi
Blue Jays general manager (1977–81)

Sportsmanship and easygoing methods are all right, but it is the prospect of a hot fight that brings out the crowds.

—John McGraw
Giants manager (1902–32)

If you're going to have a fight with a visiting club, be sure to insult them the day they come to town, and not the last day of the series. It pays off better.

—*Bill Veeck (1914–86)*
baseball executive

Who is marketing? The players are the marketing. The reason the Pirates drew two million people wasn't the fireworks or some promotion. It was winning. If the team goes bad, they don't go looking for marketing people.

—*Jack McKeon*
Padres general manager (1979–90)

You measure the value of a ballplayer by how many fannies he puts in the seats.

—*George Steinbrenner*
Yankees owner (1973–90, '93–   )

There are two classes of people whose wealth is always exaggerated by the public. They are actors and ballplayers.

—*Mike "King" Kelly*
White Sox catcher (1880–86)

People don't blink when Paul Newman gets paid millions to make a movie, or Frank Sinatra to sing. Why not a ballplayer? It's like a lot of other professions. The money is just there.

—*Ray Boone*
Tigers infielder (1953–58)

...Tom Cruise only makes one or two film appearances a year. A baseball player can be the hero or the goat one hundred sixty–two times a year.

—*Dave Winfield*
A Player's Life (1988)

If you're good enough to get into the big leagues, where you eat and sleep and travel like a millionaire and get treated like the pampered son of a millionaire wherever you go, you ought to get down on your hands and knees every day of your life and thank your God because He made you that way.

—*Mike Ryba*
Cardinals coach (1951–54)

Professional athletes are among a very small group of Americans who are able to make a lot of money when they're young. People aren't used to the idea of that, and it worries them.

—Bobby Grich
Angels infielder (1977–86)

When a man proves himself, has shown that he's a big leaguer, why I think those are the fellows should get the dough. Not some youngster who doesn't know his way into the ballpark yet.

—Lefty O'Doul
Phillies outfielder (1929–30)

I didn't ask for the money, they offered it to me. No one was ever paid more than he was worth.

—Wayne Garland
Indians pitcher (1977–81)

This league has too many .250 hitters driving Cadillacs.

—Frank Lane
White Sox general manager (1948–55)

Yankee slugger Babe Ruth: baseball's biggest box-office attraction.

A man who knows he's making money for other people ought to get some of the profit he brings in. Don't make any difference if it's baseball or a bank or a vaudeville show.

—Babe Ruth
Yankees outfielder (1920–34)

I have a hard time believing athletes are overpriced. If an owner is losing money, give it up. It's a business. I have trouble figuring out why owners would stay in if they're losing money.

—Reggie Jackson
Yankees outfielder (1977–81)

The higher a man goes up the economic scale, the less likely he is to have a nickname. . . . It's that way in baseball . . . now the players have become big money men.

—C.C. Johnson Spink
Sporting News *publisher (1962–77)*

The players I've seen making the big money may not have been the most pleasant people to get along with in the clubhouse or out on the field, but every one of those guys had one thing in common: they busted their ass when the game started.

—Jim Leyland
Pirates manager (1986–   )

Beer makes some players happy. Winning ballgames makes some players happy. Cashing checks makes me delirious with joy.

—Jim Brosnan
The Long Season (1960)

With the money I'm making, I should be playing two positions.

—Pete Rose
Phillies infielder (1979–83)

I'm the most loyal player money can buy.

—Don Sutton
Dodgers pitcher (1966–80, '88)

A homer a day will boost my pay.

—Josh Gibson
Negro Leagues catcher (1930–46)

My biggest problem in the big leagues is that I can't figure out how to spend forty–three dollars in meal money.

—Andy Van Slyke
Pirates outfielder (1987–　)

I had a problem with money. I couldn't hold on to any.

—Willie Davis
Dodgers outfielder (1960–73)

A complete ballplayer today is one who can hit, field, run, throw and pick the right agent.

—Bob Lurie
Giants owner (1976–92)

A ballplayer goes into the office now with his attorneys with him — attorneys, not one — he's got a *firm* behind him!

—Buck Leonard
Negro Leagues first baseman (1933–50)

Agents are hurting the game. So are long-term contracts. Players look at the manager and say, "Fine, Skip, say what you want, bench me if you want. I'm going to be here for five years, but you don't know where you'll be five years from now."

—*Billy Martin*
Billyball (1987)

Trade a player a year too early rather than a year too late.

—*Branch Rickey*
Dodgers general manager (1943–50)

Once you sign a contract, you're little more than cattle. If they don't want you, they can sell you or trade you, and you just moo and move along.

—*Danny Darwin*
Rangers pitcher (1978–84)

I don't think there's any loyalty in baseball at all. It's become such a transient business. If you knew you were going to be with a team ten years, then you could be loyal to a tradition. But when you know they can get rid of you tomorrow. . . .

—*Graig Nettles*
Yankees third baseman (1973–83)

Isn't it amazing that we're worth so much on the trading block and worth so little when we talk salary with the general manager?

—Jim Kern
Rangers pitcher (1979–81)

There is an old saying that money can't buy happiness. If it could, I would buy myself four hits every game.

—Pete Rose
Reds infielder (1963–79, '84–86)

Too many things seem to upset the lords of baseball, or at least the majority of them. They love to see their names in print, but want their names preceeded by the adjective "great." In that, they are not unlike the players.

—Dick Young (1918–87)
sportswriter

Baseball is a tremendous business for men with big egos. But ego can only take you so far. After that, it has to be a good business proposition.

—Brad Corbett
Rangers owner (1975–80)

When you come right down to it, the baseball owners are really little boys with big wallets.

—*Harold Parrott*
The Lords of Baseball (1976)

Whenever I got to a baseball [owner's] meeting, I never forgot to check my money and valuables at the hotel office before entering the session chamber.

—*Ferdinand Abell (1833–1913)*
baseball executive

It's a bottom line business where a lot of gray suits are brought in and then, within two years, these guys suddenly know everything about baseball.

—*Don Drysdale*
Once a Bum, Always a Dodger (1990)

Me and my owners think exactly alike. Whatever they're thinking, that's what I'm thinking.

—*Jim Fregosi*
Angels manager (1978–81)

Baseball must be a great game to survive the fools who run it.

—Bill Terry
Giants first baseman (1923–36)

Front office brilliance in baseball is rarer than a triple play.

—Roger Angell
Late Innings *(1982)*

Baseball teams are just another takeover target for corporate America. You can no more run a ballclub without thirty million dollars at your disposal than you can run for President — and never mind your qualifications for either job.

—Ron Rapoport
Chicago Sun–Times *(1985)*

National League owners are one hundred per cent for progress and one hundred per cent against change.

—Edward Bennett Williams
Orioles owner (1983–88)

Baseball is not Wall Street, it's Dream Street. It's three hours on a desert island for the guy who has to go home to a peeling tenement and a six o'clock alarm when it's over. It's the great escape, our uncommon denominator. So get the lawyers out, leave the little boys in.

—Jim Murray
Los Angeles Times *(1981)*

THE TENTH INNING

What you see here — what you hear here — let it stay here — when you leave here.

—ubiquitous sign in big-league clubhouses

Players like rules. If they didn't have any rules, they wouldn't have anything to break.

—Lee Walls
Athletics coach (1979–82)

I've never smoked or taken a drink in my life to this day. I always said you can't burn the candle at both ends. You want to be a ballplayer, be a ballplayer. If you want to go out and carouse and chase around, do that. But you can't do them both at once.

—Rube Marquard
Giants pitcher (1908–15)

Whether you want to or not, you do serve as a role model. People will always put more faith in baseball players than anyone else.

—*Brooks Robinson*
Orioles third baseman (1955–77)

When you can do it out there between the white lines, you can live any way you want.

—*Denny McLain*
Tigers pitcher (1963–70)

If I did everything they said I did, I'd be in a jar at the Harvard Medical school.

—*Bo Belinsky*
Angels pitcher (1962–64)

Hell, if I didn't drink or smoke, I'd win twenty games every year. It's easy when you don't drink or smoke or horse around.

—*Whitey Ford*
Yankees pitcher (1950, '53–67)

We led the league in card games and crossword puzzles. What happened to all the guys who drank all night, threw up all day, and went out and won ballgames?

—*Ron Kittle*
Indians outfielder (1988)

They say some of my stars drink whiskey, but I have found that the ones who drink milkshakes don't win many ballgames.

—*Casey Stengel*
Yankees manager (1949–60)

I never took the game home with me. I always left it in some bar.

—*Bob Lemon*
Yankees manager (1978–79, '81–82)

Don't drink in the hotel bar because that's where I do my drinking.

—*Casey Stengel*
Yankees manager (1949–60)

I've never played drunk. Hung over, yes, but never drunk.

> —*Hack Wilson*
> *Cubs outfielder (1926–31)*

I decided to take a page from my Dad's book. He doesn't drink, but he recommends a one–night binge to break a disastrous slump. He would do it in his own playing days. The idea is to get so wasted you can't get tied up rehashing past mistakes, and you wake up with a clean slate — in a stupor, granted, but with a clean slate.

> —*Keith Hernandez*
> *Mets first baseman (1983–89)*

Beer drinkers are always in the back of the bus. You say to yourself, they're probably back there because they're drinking beer. But beer is an acceptable part of baseball, and there is only one basic reason that beer drinkers sit in the back of the bus: it's closest to the bathroom.

> —*Tom House*
> **The Jock's Itch** *(1989)*

There is much less drinking now than there was before 1927, because I quit drinking on May 24, 1927.

—*Rabbit Maranville*
Braves shortstop (1912–20, '29–35)

Baseball players like chewing tobacco because it gives them a legitimate reason to spit. They can spit on the floor, spit at your shoes, or if they are neat, they can spit into a cup. But the idea is spitting, and what fun it is to spit.

—*Pete Franklin*
You Could Argue But You'd Be Wrong *(1988)*

Ballplayers who are first into the dining room are usually last in the averages.

—*Jimmy Cannon (1910–73)*
sportswriter

A waist is a terrible thing to mind.

—*Terry Forster*
Braves pitcher (1983–85)

Open up a ballplayer's head and you know what you'd find?
A lot of little broads and a jazz band.

—*Mayo Smith*
Tigers manager (1967–70)

Chuck Tanner used to have a bedcheck just for me every
night. No problem. My bed was always there.

—*Jim Rooker*
Pirates pitcher (1973–80)

Being with a woman all night never hurt no professional
baseball player. It's staying up all night looking for a woman
that does him in.

—*Casey Stengel*
Yankees manager (1949–60)

I'll promise to go easier on drinking and to get to bed
earlier. But not for you, fifty thousand dollars, or two hundred
fifty thousand dollars will I give up women. They're too much
fun.

—*Babe Ruth*
Yankees outfielder (1920–34)

I've seldom seen a horny player walk into a bar and not let out exactly what he did for a living.

—Johnny Bench
Reds catcher (1967–83)

I spent fifteen years honing my skills, a hundred ten bucks at a tanning salon, and thirty-five bucks having my hair styled. Then I got benched on National Secretaries Day. There is no justice.

—Bobby Grich
Angels infielder (1977–86)

Today's players don't even womanize as much as yesterday's. They don't have to . . . the women *manize.*

—Charles Einstein
Willie's Time *(1979)*

They shouldn't throw at me. I'm the father of five or six kids.

—Tito Fuentes
Giants infielder (1965–74)

We try to live good, clean lives, but whether or not we do is for our wives to judge.

—*Bob Dernier*
Cubs outfielder (1984–87)

All this intellectual slobbering over a game slightly duller than watching Jell–O set reminds me of the time an especially precious baseball writer was sitting in a dugout with an old, randomly toothed coach, looking out on two stars as they stood talking side by side in the outfield. "You know," said the writer. . . . "It must be something to share in the comraderie of the game, to discuss the plan of battle, to share the oneness of the team, to steel themselves for the daily taste of sweetness or bitterness."

The coach lobbed a wad of tobacco juice onto the dugout floor. "Nah," he said. "Probably talkin' about a broad."

—*Rick Reilly*
Sports Illustrated *(1991)*

BASEBALL GEOGRAPHY: THE AMERICAN LEAGUE

BALTIMORE ORIOLES

The Baltimore Orioles are, and always have been just a superbly run organization which sends up young control pitchers and complete if unspectacular ballplayers with assembly-line regularity.

—*Tim Burke*
Montreal Gazette *(1983)*

Baltimore's such a lousy town, Francis Scott Key went out in a boat to write "The Star Spangled Banner."

—*Billy Martin*
Yankees manager (1975–79, '83, '85, '88)

The splendor of Oriole Park is in its character and details. It is built of brick and steel, not the concrete like the flying saucers that landed in too many major league cities starting about 25 years ago. . . . As you squint in the sunlight, there is a sense that you've already seen a thousand games in this place . . . it's as if this ballpark comes equipped with memories.

Tim Kurkjian
Sports Illustrated *(1992)*

This was a town that God forgot since Wilbert Robinson, John McGraw and Willie Keeler left. You can't tell Sunday from Saturday. You can't tell one residence from another. . . . How a drunk ever finds his own house at night, nobody ever knows, unless he has his own personal St. Bernard.

—Furman Bisher
"The Town that God Forgot" (1966)

Shortstop Cal Ripken, Jr., the son of the Orioles' longtime third base coach, enjoys a distinct Baltimore pedigree.

In the only sport where the team on defense has the ball, the Orioles are unmatched in thinking until it hurts, taking hard aim at a foe's soft spots and intimidating in a graceful, almost subtle manner.

—*Bob Verdi*
Chicago Tribune (1983)

BOSTON RED SOX

Baseball isn't a life and death matter, but the Red Sox are.

—*Mike Barnicle*
Boston Globe (1978)

In Boston, we believe, and we are never disappointed because what we believe is this: the world will break your heart someday, and we are luckier than most — we get ours broken every year, at Fenway Park

—*George V. Higgins*
"Fenway, with Tears" (1979)

The Red Sox in my immature mind were like the man in the Hollywood movie who, because he's wearing a tuxedo, is bound to slip on a banana peel. They were gallantry and grace without the crassness of victory.

—John Updike
"Loving the Sox" (1986)

There's nothing in the world like the fatalism of the Red Sox fans, which has been bred into them for generations by that little green ballpark, and by The Wall, and by a team that keeps trying to win by hitting everything out of sight and just out-bombarding everyone else in the league. All this makes Boston fans a little crazy. I'm sorry for them.

—Bill Lee
Red Sox pitcher (1969–78)

The Great Wall of Boston, the left field fence, the Tombstone of the Red Sox. It has done more to bury their pennant chances year in and year out than the generations of scatter-arm shortstops, banjo hitters, crooked-arm pitchers and even the unfriendly press. The Wall is the biggest enemy to Boston since the Redcoats.

—Jim Murray
Los Angeles Times (1967)

The Red Sox truly are the boys of summer; it's always been the fall that's given them trouble.

—*Dan Shaughnessy*
Curse of the Bambino (1990)

CALIFORNIA ANGELS

The Angels are a different lot. While the Dodgers have a long and rich history, the Angels' is short and sour, and filled with disappointments. If they somehow make the playoffs, it's only to find a new way to lose. Usually though, they don't even get that chance.

—*Bob Wood*
Dodger Dogs to Fenway Franks (1988)

They're like the American League all-star team, and that's their problem. The American League all-star team always loses.

—*Dan Quisenberry*
Royals pitcher (1979–88)

Money isn't everything. Look at the California Angels.

—Jim Murray
Los Angeles Times *(1978)*

The way they dress here, your head is always in the stands. All those bikinis — your eyes get tired.

—Rod Carew
Angels first baseman (1979–85)

CHICAGO WHITE SOX

It's different being a White Sox fan. Bill Veeck once wrote, "If there is any justice in this world, to be a White Sox fan frees a man from any other form of penance." And it might be added, pennants.

—Bob Vanderberg
From Lane and Fain to Zisk and Fisk *(1982)*

If I was going to storm a pillbox, going to sheer, utter certain death and the colonel said, "Shepherd, pick six guys," I'd pick six White Sox fans, because they have known death every day of their lives and it holds no terror for them.

—*Jean Shepherd (b. 1929)*
humorist

Things were so bad in Chicago last summer that by the fifth inning we were selling hot dogs to go.

—*Ken Brett*
White Sox pitcher (1976–77)

South Siders are creatures of habit. . . . what they want is the same neighborhoods, the same schools, the same mayor in office for twenty years, and the same family baseball tradition for eighty years.

—*Bob Logan*
Miracle on 33rd Street (1984)

If a man tells you he's a fan of both the White Sox and the Cubs, check your wallet, make sure your watch is still on your wrist, and lock your car doors. It doesn't work that way in Chicago.

—*Jay Johnstone*
Temporary Insanity (1985)

CLEVELAND INDIANS

We are now arriving in Cleveland. Set back your watches forty-two minutes.

—Tim McCarver
Red Sox catcher (1974–75)

If you're going to have a plane crash in Cleveland, it's better to have one on the way in than on the way out.

—Peter Gammons
Boston Globe (1983)

In Cleveland, pennant fever usually ends up being just a forty-eight-hour virus.

—Frank Robinson
Indians manager (1975–77)

If you're a thirty-five-year-old Cleveland fan who started following the team when you were ten, you must be pretty fed up by now. You haven't had a good September in your life.

—Bruce Jenkins
Life After Saberhagen (1986)

Cleveland's Municipal Stadium . . . is a monument to architectural homeliness. Vastness is its only virtue. When it is empty, there is no greater emptiness.

—Jane Leavy
Squeeze Play (1990)

There's nothing wrong with this stadium that a case of dynamite couldn't cure.

—Mike Hargrove
Indians first baseman (1979–85)

The first thing they do in Cleveland, if you have talent, is trade you for three guys who don't.

—Jim Kern
Indians pitcher (1974–78, '86)

The Cleveland Indians are baseball's first bionic baseball team … a team assembled from the living scraps and donated parts of other baseball teams, without a heart or a soul or a reason for living, that you can tell.

—Bill James
Baseball Abstract (1983)

The only good thing about playing in Cleveland is you don't have to make the road trips there.

—*Richie Scheinblum*
Indians outfielder (1965, '67–69)

A three-time loser is a baseball manager on his way to Cleveland in an Edsel.

—*Bobby Bragan*
Indians manager (1958)

DETROIT TIGERS

Some people laugh at us. They poke all kinds of fun at Detroit. We're right up there with Buffalo and Cleveland on the joke list. Maybe we've even taken over the top spot. Ever see a travel poster inviting you to visit Detroit on vacation?

—*Joe Falls*
The Detroit Tigers *(1989)*

To first glance at Tiger Stadium was one of my all-time favorite thrills. The place glowed. . . . Perched up over the highway, its light standards thrust high above like castle towers, it was a palace amid the rubble of the city.

—Bob Wood
Dodger Dogs to Fenway Franks *(1988)*

Opening Day in Detroit is to baseball what Easter is to church. The faithful come out, but a lot of once-a-year attendees are there too.

—Ernie Harwell
Tuned to Baseball *(1985)*

Detroit is a great town. I like it. I've bought a home here and have roots here. But the fans in this town are the worst in the league . . . . if they think we're stupid for playing this game, how stupid are they for watching us?

—Denny McLain
Tigers pitcher (1963–70)

KANSAS CITY ROYALS

[Royals Stadium] is actually not such a bad ballpark. The problem with it is that ever since it was built in 1973, it has become the Golden Arches of baseball. Considered perfect by architects and teams, it has been cloned and packaged like fast food, for quick delivery to any city desiring a new franchise . . . .

Philip Lowry
Green Cathedrals (1992)

Like any Holiday Inn, the stadium appears forever new, and thus without history — the wrong overtones for a sport so devotedly attached to its ancestors and its family records.

—Roger Angell
Late Innings (1982)

They're loyal Royal all the way. But they're not tough fans . . . a player doesn't have to worry about being insulted there.

—Sparky Anderson
Tigers manager (1979–   )

The city's image would improve a lot if they would just accept themselves for what they are, and stop handing out malarkey about how many miles of boulevard they have … Kansas City has a world-class inferiority complex, but they also have a world-class ballclub.

—*Bill James*
Baseball Abstract *(1985)*

MILWAUKEE BREWERS

They know when to cheer, and they know when to boo. And they know when to drink beer. They do it all the time.

—*Gorman Thomas*
Brewers outfielder (1973–83, '86)

I don't want to hear another bleeping question from you. Milwaukee, don't print that. I don't want the people back there to think I swear.

—*Harvey Kuenn*
Brewers manager (1975, '82–83)

MINNESOTA TWINS

This region has long had America's friendliest and most unashamedly fickle fans. They enjoy, but do not trust, victory. They endure, but do not truly suffer from, defeat.

—*Thomas Boswell*
The Heart of the Order *(1989)*

Baseball is baseball, except in the Dome. It ain't baseball here.

—*Ron Davis*
Twins pitcher *(1982–86)*

Ever see a ground ball lost in the lights—in the daytime? . . . the roof is about the same color as a baseball. It's the only place in the big leagues where an outfielder can say, "I lost it in the Teflon."

—*Bruce Jenkins*
Life After Saberhagen *(1986)*

NEW YORK YANKEES

We're loved and hated, but always in larger doses than any other teams. We're the only team in any sport whose name and uniform and insignia are synonymous with the entire sport all over the world. When you're with any other team, you have to accept it; but the Yankees mean baseball to more people than all the other teams combined.

—Paul Blair
Yankees outfielder (1977–80)

As much as we disliked the Yankees — fans and players alike — they were good for baseball. . . . The consistently unsuccessful teams like the Browns, Senators and A's paid a lot of their bills with those big crowds that poured through the gates when the Yankees came to town.

—Bob Feller
Indians pitcher (1936–41, '45–56)

They don't just beat you. They break your heart.

—Joe Judge
Senators first baseman (1915–32)

The Yankee pinstripes, they stay with you wherever you go. To me, being a Yankee always meant playing with pride, desire, self-confidence, the will to win.

—Billy Martin
Yankees manager (1975–79, '83, '85, '88)

It may be noted that the Yankees are the least popular of all baseball clubs, because they win, which leaves nothing to "if" about.

—A.J. Liebling (1904–63)
columnist

The Yankees, we suppose, are forever. They are stern and cold and untouched by common colds and flat tires and backaches like the rest of us common folk.

—Blackie Sherrod
Dallas Times Herald *(1963)*

Yankee Stadium, where triumph was cheap and tragedy nonexistent.

—*Leonard Schecter*
Once upon the Polo Grounds (1970)

Rooting for the Yankees is like rooting for U.S. Steel.

—*Joe E. Lewis (1902–71)*
comedian

The more self-centered and egotistical a guy is, the better ballplayer he's going to be. You take a team with twenty-five assholes and I'll show you a pennant. I'll show you the New York Yankees.

—*Bill Lee*
Red Sox pitcher (1969–78)

The Yankees, too, are family. A family like the Macbeths, the Borgias and the Bordens of Fall River, Massachusetts.

—*Ron Fimrite*
Sports Illustrated (1979)

Hating the Yankees is as American as pizza pie, unwed mothers and cheating on your income tax.

—*Mike Royko*
Chicago Sun–Times *(1977)*

A Yankee fan is a complacent, ignorant fat cat. He knows nothing about baseball except that the Yankees will win the pennant and the World Series more often than they won't and that a home run is the only gesture of any worth in the entire game.

—*Arnold Hano*
A Day in the Bleachers *(1955)*

I could never play in New York. The first time I ever came into a game there, I got into the bullpen car and they told me to lock the doors.

—*Mike Flanagan*
Orioles pitcher *(1975–87)*

When I was a little boy, I wanted to be a baseball player and join the circus. With the Yankees I've accomplished both.

—*Graig Nettles*
Yankees third baseman (1973–83)

OAKLAND ATHLETICS

Tony Bennett never left his heart in Oakland. In fact, he probably did as much as he could to avoid even entering its filthy city limits. Oakland seems more a sister to a hole like Cleveland than the "City by the Golden Gate." Simply put, Oakland is a dive.

—*Bob Wood*
Dodger Dogs to Fenway Franks *(1988)*

I have never been a great admirer of the Oakland Coliseum. A's captain Sal Bando got it right when he dubbed that too-symmetric, no-frills, basic concrete ring "The Mausoleum."

—*John Krich*
"Blues for a Lost October" (1989)

Some people asked me if I would be interested in managing the A's. I said a definite no, thank you. At night, that place is a graveyard with lights.

—Whitey Herzog
Cardinals manager (1980–90)

SEATTLE MARINERS

Seattle, a thriving metropolis that *Places Rated Almanac* cites as the best place to live in America. Perhaps to even things out, Seattle also has the Mariners.

—Jim Street
"Lost at Sea" (1990)

Playing in Seattle was like playing for Mr. Rogers in the beautiful neighborhood, very low-key, tranquil. The fans were polite and applauded. But Seattle was not a contending team. . . . It was as though Seattle didn't register with the rest of America as a major league franchise.

—Lenny Randle
Mariners infielder (1981–82)

Seattle provides as much tradition to the game as might be found in downtown Moscow. . . . As a town it neither understands nor supports the game, all the while insisting on its right to keep it.

—Bob Wood
Dodger Dogs to Fenway Franks (1988)

The Seattle Mariners tried a novel promotion gimmick Saturday night — winning.

—E.M. Swift
Sports Illustrated (1981)

Being named manager of the Seattle Mariners is like becoming head chef at McDonald's.

—Charles Bricker
San Jose Mercury (1981)

When the end of the world comes, Seattle will still have one more year to go.

—Dick Vertlieb
Mariners general manager (1977–81)

TEXAS RANGERS

The Rangers (*nee* Senators) American League franchise — quite arguably the most disappointing and uninspired in baseball's long history — has been repeatedly characterized from the earliest years by a ceaseless parade of bungling, egotistical owners, disastrous trades and inexplicable personnel moves, remarkably inept yearly play and little support from the baseball faithful in two consistently-abused big league cities.

—Peter C. Bjarkman
Encyclopedia of Baseball Team Histories: American League *(1991)*

The Rangers have a history of folding in July — about the time when the Arlington grass turns brown.

—Craig R. Wright
STATS Annual *(1990)*

Even if our people are enthused, which they don't seem to be, it's too damned hot to go to the ballpark!

—Blackie Sherrod
Dallas Times Herald *(1972)*

Before the 1987 season, Rangers veteran Larry Parrish said that "people expect the labor pains to be over. They expect to see the baby." It was an ugly baby from the first squall.

—*Bill James*
Baseball Abstract *(1988)*

TORONTO BLUE JAYS

Except for being a little cleaner, a little quieter, and a lot safer than most major league cities, Toronto could just as easily be stamped "Made in the USA." Its culture, while a foreign one, is red, white and blue all about the edges.

—*Bob Wood*
Dodger Dogs to Fenway Franks *(1988)*

Whenever the Blue Jays play, both American and Canadian anthems are played.... If each anthem averages a minute and a half, players for Canadian teams spend a full eight hours listening to anthems in the course of a hundred sixty-two game season — a working day's worth of phony patriotism.

—*Alison Gordon*
Foul Ball! *(1984)*

WASHINGTON SENATORS

For the Washington Senators, the worst time of the year is the baseball season.

—Roger Kahn (b. 1927)
sportswriter

There is a federal law that forbids them to win.

—John Steinbeck (1902–68)
author

Watching the Washington Senators, you forget the beauty of baseball. You forget the bare-handed grab, the elegant stretch at first, the choreography of a six-four-three double play. Watching the Washington Senators is like watching the human condition without the slapstick. It is an exercise in humility.

—Jane Leavy
Squeeze Play *(1990)*

The Senators might have been one of baseball's most god-awful teams, a threadbare and lackluster group of has-beens, never-wases, and names that were not even household names in their own households.

—*Bert Randolph Sugar*
Baseballistics (1990)

We cheer for the Senators, we pray for the Senators, and we hope that the Supreme Court doesn't declare them unconstitutional.

—*Lyndon B. Johnson (1908–73)*
36th President of the United States

From the Taft Administration through the time of the team's departure from Washington, D.C. in 1971, the President threw out the first ball for the Senators on Opening Day. It was the only time the Senators weren't in last place.

BASEBALL GEOGRAPHY: THE NATIONAL LEAGUE

ATLANTA BRAVES

If failure in baseball were fatal, the Atlanta Braves would have died a long time ago. Since moving to Atlanta from Milwaukee in 1966, the Braves have had the worst record in the major leagues.

—Bob Hope
We Could've Finished Last Without You *(1991)*

The Atlanta Braves are in last place, where they have been for the last four years. I wonder if they signed a lease?

—Hank Greenwald
Giants broadcaster

Fans out here say there are only two seasons — fall football and spring football.

—Steve Stone
Cubs broadcaster (1979–86, '89–   )

BROOKLYN DODGERS

In Brooklyn, it was as though you were in your own little bubble . . . you were all part of one big but very close family, and the Dodgers were the main topic of everybody's conversations . . . you could sense the affection people had for you. I don't know that such a thing exists anymore.

—Don Drysdale
Once a Bum, Always a Dodger (1990)

The baseball team in Brooklyn has been and is a needle to deflate Manhattan, to irritate the proud who walk and work and live among the soaring, boastful towers that dominate the skyline.

—Red Barber
introduction to **Dodger Daze and Knights (1953)**

It was Brooklyn against the world. They were not only complete fanatics, but they knew baseball like the fans of no other city. It was exciting to play there. It was a treat. I walked into that crummy, flyblown park as Brooklyn manager for nine years, and every time I entered, my pulse quickened and my spirits soared.

—*Leo Durocher*
Dodgers manager (1939–46, '48)

The field was even greener than my boy's mind had pictured it. In later years, friends of ours visited Ireland and said the grass there was plenty green all right, but that not even the Emerald Isle itself was as green as the grass that grew in Ebbets Field.

—*Duke Snider*
The Duke of Flatbush *(1988)*

The noise level at the park produced earaches. It spilled out onto Bedford Avenue and into the surrounding neighborhood. It was possible five blocks away to tell if the Dodgers were doing well or not in a particular game by the rise and fall of the sounds.

—*Harvey Frommer*
New York City Baseball *(1985)*

Even when they lose, they got heart. That's why the people of Brooklyn love 'em so much. Now if only those crooked politicians running this borough had half the brains of those baseball players, we'd be in a lot better shape.

—David Ritz
The Man Who Brought the Dodgers Back to Brooklyn *(1981)*

CHICAGO CUBS

Every player should be accorded the privilege of at least one season with the Chicago Cubs. That's baseball as it should be played — in God's own sunshine. And that's really living.

—Alvin Dark
Cubs infielder (1958–59)

Wrigley Field — a Renaissance museum of baseball, the Florence of the major leagues.

—Jerry Klinkowitz
"Playing the Game at Wrigley Field" (1987)

I'd play for half my salary if I could hit in this dump [Wrigley] all the time.

—*Babe Ruth*
Yankees outfielder (1920–34)

Owned by the *Chicago Tribune*, the Cubs are sports' answer to the typographical error. Even referring to the Cubs as a baseball team leaves you open to libel.

—*Art Spander*
San Francisco Examiner (1983)

Ronald Reagan has had the two most demanding jobs in the country — President of the United States and radio broadcaster for the Chicago Cubs.

—*George Will*
author (1981)

The Chicago Cubs are like Rush Street — a lot of singles, but no action.

—*Joe Garagiola*
Cubs catcher (1953–54)

The Cubs are into their thirty-sixth rebuilding year.

—Joe Goddard
Chicago Sun–Times *(1981)*

Other teams won and made it look easy. The Cubs lost and made it look hard.

—David Brinkley
newscaster (1981)

CINCINNATI REDS

If there is a single place that is baseball's podium, from which the game's enthralling, labyrinthine narrative has been delivered, it is Cincinnati. . . . And if there is one city whose removal from the face of baseball history would disfeature it beyond redemption, it is Cincinnati.

—Lonnie Wheeler and John Baskin
The Cincinnati Game *(1988)*

Cincinnati is nuts with baseball! They ought to call this town Cincinnutty!

—Arthur "Bugs" Baer
sportswriter (1919)

The Cincinnati fan is conservative. The good burghers give the visiting player the impression that, "You told me to save my money and come out and watch you, and look how you play."

—*Joe Garagiola*
Baseball Is a Funny Game *(1960)*

Did you ever hear anyone bragging about Cincinnati being a good town? It's the only city in the country where the locals are absolutely neutral.

—*Jimmy Cannon (1910–73)*
sportswriter

Crosley Field was like the private sanctuary of the people of Cincinnati. It had intensity. You could feel the reaction and the pulsations of the crowd. At Riverfront, it's more like going into a very large business and watching progress.

—*Waite Hoyt*
Reds broadcaster (1942–65)

HOUSTON ASTROS

Texas has a rather confusing image. It's the country of rugged outdoors people, where they play baseball and football under a roof.

—Bill Vaughn
Half the Battle (1967)

This is the only town where women wear insect repellent instead of perfume.

—Richie Ashburn
Phillies broadcaster (1963–   )

Of the three, Minnesota's funny-looking bubbletop, Seattle's concrete tombstone and Houston's, the Astrodome is easily the most handsome. Even so, that's like pitting Quasimodo, Frankenstein and the Phantom of the Opera against each other in a beauty contest. Domes compare only with domes.

—Bob Wood
Dodger Dogs to Fenway Franks (1988)

The Houston Astrodome is the biggest hairdryer in the world.

—*Joe Pepitone*
Astros first baseman (1970)

No one booed an Astro player. No one got into a fight; a fight at the Astrodome would be as shocking as fisticuffs in the College of Cardinals.

—*Roger Angell*
The Summer Game (1972)

The Astros take the field and you're nauseous. Those uniforms . . . blue, yellow and burnt orange, mixed into a hideous rainbow going right across the chest, it's the uniform that won't leave, a long-standing joke that keeps coming back. You're thinking, maybe that's why the Astros have never made it to the World Series; they have no taste.

—*Bruce Jenkins*
Life After Saberhagen (1986)

LOS ANGELES DODGERS

The Los Angeles Dodgers are a first-class operation, but their blue-blooded arrogance is a royal pain . . . the Dodgers are the smartest kid in the class, the yuppie with the latest car phone, the golfer with the new pings.

—Mark Whicker
"The Franchise You Love to Hate" (1990)

There's magic in the Dodger uniform.

—Jimmy Wynn
Dodgers outfielder (1974–75)

The [L.A.] girls all look like Bridgitte Bardot. Come to think of it, some of the men do, too.

—Jim Murray
Los Angeles Times (1965)

You know that scene in the movie *Gandhi* with a cast of thousands marching to the sea? It was filmed outside Dodger Stadium in the bottom of the seventh. . . . People here don't believe the axiom about a ballgame never being over until the last out. That's because they've never seen the last out.

—*Art Spander*
San Francisco Examiner (1982)

Baseball out here in L.A. is too laid back. Instead of a coach, the Dodgers have a third base shrink. And too mellow? Who ever heard of a game being called because of bad karma?

—*Johnny Carson (b. 1925)*
Tonight Show *host*

MONTREAL EXPOS

Baseball remains a popular game here, in spite of the Expos, but hockey is the way of life.

—*Mordecai Richler*
"Up from the Minors in Montreal" (1979)

The modern-day player doesn't hate Montreal so much as he's afraid of it. He's afraid that people who have gotten along for hundreds of years without him will criticize him in a language he doesn't understand.

> —*Dick Williams*
> *Expos manager (1977–81)*

They discovered "boo" is pronounced the same in French as it is in English.

> —*Harry Caray (b. 1920)*
> *Cubs broadcaster*

NEW YORK METS

There is more Met than Yankee in every one of us.

> —*Roger Kahn (b. 1927)*
> *author*

They've shown me ways to lose I never knew existed.

> —*Casey Stengel*
> *Mets manager (1962–65)*

I have a son and I make him watch the Mets. I want him to know life. It's a history lesson. He'll understand the depression.

—*Toots Shor (1904–1977)*
restaurateur

The whole Shea Stadium thing, the planes going over, the fans yelling and screaming — and there's just as many unknowledgeable fans in New York as anywhere else. I love to play the Mets because you have to enjoy the competition. No one in the division roots for the Mets.

—*Buck Rodgers*
Expos manager (1985–91)

PHILADELPHIA PHILLIES

If you're associated with the Philadelphia media or town, you look for negatives . . . I don't know if there's something about their upbringing or they have too many hoagies, too much cream cheese.

—*Mike Schmidt*
Phillies third baseman (1972–89)

Third baseman Mike Schmidt—the target of Quaker City boobirds, and the greatest player in Phillies history.

Baseball fans make a number of strange sounds, but the only one that has been isolated and genetically identified with the game is the sound, "boo." And the home of the boo, its very Cooperstown, is Philadelphia.

—Wilfrid Sheed
"Mr. Mack and the Main Chance" (1979)

Philadelphia fans would boo funerals, an Easter egg hunt, a parade of armless war vets and the Liberty Bell.

—Bo Belinsky
Phillies pitcher (1965–66)

The cops picked me up on the street at three A.M. and fined me five hundred dollars for being drunk and one hundred dollars for being with the Phillies.

—Bob Uecker
Phillies catcher (1966–67)

On a clear day, they could see seventh place.

—Fresco Thompson
Phillies infielder (1927–30)

PITTSBURGH PIRATES

Pittsburgh is such a tough town; even the canaries sing bass there.

—*Arthur "Bugs" Baer (1886–1969)*
sportswriter

[People in Pittsburgh] are not baseball fans. It gets awfully lonesome playing before five thousand and six thousand even when you're in a pennant race. They come out of all those dirty mines and blast furnaces, and all they want to do is grab a cold beer and see people beat up on each other. They're more football fans.

—*Bill Madlock*
Pirates infielder (1979–85)

In Pittsburgh, [owner] Barney Dreyfuss has arranged his refreshment layout so that it is the first thing seen by incoming fans. His is the only stand where the customer has to buy hot dog and hamburger tickets in advance.

—*Boseman Bulger*
New York Evening World (1927)

Frankly, the fans who come out are dedicated fans. I can almost remember them by name.

—Dave Parker
Pirates outfielder (1973–83)

ST. LOUIS CARDINALS

With respect to my home city of St. Louis, we once proudly had the title, "first in booze, first in shoes and last in the American League." We lost our American League team. Our shoes went to Taiwan and Korea. God, do not take from us our beer.

—Thomas Eagleton (b. 1929)
U.S. Senator

St. Louis is baseball All-American style. Not like Philly. Not like New York. Not like anywhere else. In St. Louis, the fans care about the game . . . . Here they talked strategy — the hit-and-run, the squeeze play, the defensive alignment . . . the fans didn't care about off-field controversies.

—Dick Allen
Cardinals infielder (1970)

St. Louis, boy did it ever get hot there. Jeez, you'd roast out on that field, and the nights were just as bad. Try to sleep and before you know it you were lying in a pool of water.

—Lefty O'Doul
Phillies outfielder (1929–30)

You ever been in St. Looie in July? You come up to bat with sweat bustin' from your ears. You step up an' look out there to where the pitcher oughta be, an' you see four of him . . . . they got it all growed out in grass in April, but after July First — it's paved with concrete!

—Thomas Wolfe
You Can't Go Home Again *(1940)*

Has anyone beside me noticed how boring the St. Louis Cardinals are? They don't win, they just kind of swarm. You should spray 'em, not play 'em.

—Jim Murray
Los Angeles Times *(1982)*

SAN DIEGO PADRES

Every season it's predicted that the Padres are about to go somewhere. And every year it turns out to be the beach.

—*Thomas Boswell*
Washington Post *(1984)*

We've got a whole bunch of new players. But I don't think they're the right ones.

—*Ozzie Smith*
Padres shortstop (1978–81)

This was a franchise that had behaved like they were managed by a television announcer. Oh yeah — they were. Jerry Coleman bossed them in 1980. They say he was late for a spring workout that year because he was busy filming a car commercial. Since then, the team had become an Alka–Seltzer commercial.

—*Dick Williams*
Padres manager (1982–85)

The club is a helluva lot of fun, like my wife, but there's no profit in either one.

—*Ray Kroc*
Padres owner (1973–83)

SAN FRANCISCO GIANTS

A business executive is standing in his office looking down over the city . . . . suddenly a falling figure shoots past the window. "Uh oh," the man says, glancing at his chronometer. "It must be June. There go the Giants."

—*Jim Murray*
Los Angeles Times *(1965)*

A Candlestick crowd . . . is conspicuous for its groups of raging, drunken, unaccompanied white male bozos. It's a nine-inning episode of *Animal House* in which the food fights and fist fights prove far more compelling than anything happening on the field.

—*John Krich*
"Blues for a Lost October" (1989)

This wouldn't be such a bad place to play if it wasn't for the wind. I guess that's like saying hell wouldn't be such a bad place if it wasn't so hot.

—Jerry Reuss
Dodgers pitcher (1979–87)

Candlestick Park is the gross error in the history of major league baseball. Designed at a corner table in Lefty O'Doul's, a Frisco saloon, by two politicians and an itinerant ditchdigger, the ballpark slants toward the bay — in fact it *slides* toward the bay and before long it'll be underwater, which is the best place for it.

—Jim Brosnan
Pennant Race (1962)

Batting in Candlestick is like trying to hit a cotton ball wearing an overcoat.

—Bill Madlock
Giants infielder (1977–79)

Candlestick Park. That's the ninth blunder of the world.

—Herb Caen
San Francisco Chronicle (1980)

The only difference between Candlestick and San Quentin is that at Candlestick they let you go home at night.

—Jim Wohlford
Giants outfielder (1980–82)

ALL-TIME FRANCHISE
ALL-STAR TEAMS

In 1993, the National League expanded to 14 teams, with the addition of the Colorado Rockies and Florida Marlins. This evened the N.L.'s total team count with that of the American League, which has fielded 14 clubs since 1977.

Excluding the fledgling Rockies and Marlins, here's one man's selections for all-time teams of the 26 other big league ballclubs. These "dream squads" include players at the eight regular positions, along with a starting pitcher (SP), relief pitcher (RP) and each franchise's all-time best skipper (MGR). Let the arguments commence.

THE NATIONAL LEAGUE

ASTROS

C	Alan Ashby
1B	Bob Watson
2B	Bill Doran
SS	Roger Metzger
3B	Doug Rader
OF	Jose Cruz
OF	Cesar Cedeno
OF	Jim Wynn
SP	Mike Scott
RP	Dave Smith
MGR	Bill Virdon

BRAVES

C	Del Crandall
1B	Joe Adcock
2B	Felix Millan
SS	Rabbit Maranville
3B	Eddie Mathews
OF	Ralph Garr
OF	Dale Murphy
OF	Henry Aaron
SP	Warren Spahn
RP	Gene Garber
MGR	Fred Haney

CARDINALS

C	Ted Simmons
1B	Jim Bottomley
2B	Rogers Hornsby
SS	Ozzie Smith
3B	Ken Boyer
OF	Lou Brock
OF	Enos Slaughter
OF	Stan Musial
SP	Bob Gibson
RP	Bruce Sutter
MGR	Whitey Herzog

CUBS

C	Gabby Hartnett
1B	Frank Chance
2B	Ryne Sandberg
SS	Ernie Banks
3B	Ron Santo
OF	Riggs Stephenson
OF	Billy Williams
OF	Hack Wilson
SP	Mordecai Brown
RP	Lee Smith
MGR	Charlie Grimm

DODGERS

C	Roy Campanella
1B	Gil Hodges
2B	Jackie Robinson
SS	Pee Wee Reese
3B	Ron Cey
OF	Zack Wheat
OF	Duke Snider
OF	Carl Furillo
SP	Sandy Koufax
RP	Ron Perranoski
MGR	Walter Alston

EXPOS

C	Gary Carter
1B	Andres Gallaraga
2B	Delino DeShields
SS	Tim Foli
3B	Tim Wallach
OF	Tim Raines
OF	Andre Dawson
OF	Rusty Staub
SP	Steve Rogers
RP	Jeff Reardon
MGR	Buck Rodgers

GIANTS

C	Tom Haller
1B	Bill Terry
2B	Frankie Frisch
SS	Travis Jackson
3B	Fred Lindstrom
OF	Willie McCovey
OF	Willie Mays
OF	Mel Ott
SP	Christy Mathewson
RP	Greg Minton
MGR	John McGraw

METS

C	Jerry Grote
1B	Ed Kranepool
2B	Ron Hunt
SS	Bud Harrelson
3B	Howard Johnson
OF	Cleon Jones
OF	Lee Mazzilli
OF	Darryl Strawberry
SP	Tom Seaver
RP	Jesse Orosco
MGR	Davey Johnson

PADRES

C	Benito Santiago
1B	Nate Colbert
2B	Alan Wiggins
SS	Garry Templeton
3B	Graig Nettles
OF	Gene Richards
OF	Tony Gwynn
OF	Dave Winfield
SP	Randy Jones
RP	Rollie Fingers
MGR	Dick Williams

PHILLIES

C	Bob Boone
1B	Don Hurst
2B	Manny Trillo
SS	Larry Bowa
3B	Mike Schmidt
OF	Chuck Klein
OF	Richie Ashburn
OF	Del Ennis
SP	Robin Roberts
RP	Tug McGraw
MGR	Gene Mauch

PIRATES

C	Tony Pena
1B	Willie Stargell
2B	Bill Mazeroski
SS	Honus Wagner
3B	Pie Traynor
OF	Ralph Kiner
OF	Paul Waner
OF	Roberto Clemente
SP	Bob Friend
RP	Kent Tekulve
MGR	Danny Murtaugh

REDS

C	Johnny Bench
1B	Tony Perez
2B	Joe Morgan
SS	Dave Concepcion
3B	Pete Rose
OF	Edd Roush
OF	Vada Pinson
OF	Frank Robinson
SP	Eppa Rixey
RP	John Franco
MGR	Sparky Anderson

THE AMERICAN LEAGUE

ANGELS

C	Bob Rodgers
1B	Wally Joyner
2B	Bobby Grich
SS	Jim Fregosi
3B	Doug DeCinces
OF	Brian Downing
OF	Don Baylor
OF	Leon Wagner
SP	Nolan Ryan
RP	Bryan Harvey
MGR	Bill Rigney

ATHLETICS

C	Mickey Cochrane
1B	Jimmie Foxx
2B	Eddie Collins
SS	Bert Campaneris
3B	Frank "Home Run" Baker
OF	Al Simmons
OF	Rickey Henderson
OF	Reggie Jackson
SP	Lefty Grove
RP	Dennis Eckersley
MGR	Connie Mack

BLUE JAYS

C	Ernie Whitt
1B	Willie Upshaw
2B	Roberto Alomar
SS	Tony Fernandez
3B	Kelly Gruber
OF	George Bell
OF	Lloyd Moseby
OF	Jesse Barfield
SP	Dave Stieb
RP	Tom Henke
MGR	Cito Gaston

BREWERS

C	B.J. Surhoff
1B	Cecil Cooper
2B	Paul Molitor
SS	Robin Yount
3B	Don Money
OF	Ben Oglivie
OF	Gorman Thomas
OF	Larry Hisle
SP	Mike Caldwell
RP	Dan Plesac
MGR	Harvey Kuenn

INDIANS

C	Jim Hegan
1B	Hal Trosky
2B	Nap Lajoie
SS	Lou Boudreau
3B	Al Rosen
OF	Larry Doby
OF	Tris Speaker
OF	Rocky Colavito
SP	Bob Feller
RP	Doug Jones
MGR	Lou Boudreau

MARINERS

C	Dave Valle
1B	Alvin Davis
2B	Harold Reynolds
SS	Spike Owen
3B	Edgar Martinez
OF	Richie Zisk
OF	Ken Griffey, Jr.
OF	Phil Bradley
SP	Mark Langston
RP	Mike Schooler
MGR	Jim Lefebvre

ORIOLES

C	Gus Triandos
1B	Eddie Murray
2B	Rich Dauer
SS	Cal Ripken, Jr.
3B	Brooks Robinson
OF	Frank Robinson
OF	Paul Blair
OF	Ken Singleton
SP	Jim Palmer
RP	Tippy Martinez
MGR	Earl Weaver

RANGERS

C	Jim Sundberg
1B	Mike Hargrove
2B	Julio Franco
SS	Toby Harrah
3B	Buddy Bell
OF	Jeff Burroughs
OF	Ruben Sierra
OF	Al Oliver
SP	Charlie Hough
RP	Jeff Russell
MGR	Bobby Valentine

RED SOX

C	Carlton Fisk
1B	George Scott
2B	Bobby Doerr
SS	Joe Cronin
3B	Wade Boggs
OF	Ted Williams
OF	Jim Rice
OF	Carl Yastrzemski
SP	Cy Young
RP	Dick Radatz
MGR	Joe Cronin

ROYALS

C	Darrell Porter
1B	John Mayberry
2B	Frank White
SS	Fred Patek
3B	George Brett
OF	Hal McRae
OF	Willie Wilson
OF	Amos Otis
SP	Dennis Leonard
RP	Dan Quisenberry
MGR	Dick Howser

TIGERS

C	Bill Freehan
1B	Hank Greenberg
2B	Charlie Gehringer
SS	Alan Trammell
3B	George Kell
OF	Ty Cobb
OF	Harry Heilmann
OF	Al Kaline
SP	Jack Morris
RP	John Hiller
MGR	Steve O'Neill

TWINS

C	Butch Wynegar
1B	Kent Hrbek
2B	Rod Carew
SS	Greg Gagne
3B	Harmon Killebrew
OF	Bob Allison
OF	Kirby Puckett
OF	Tony Oliva
SP	Jim Kaat
RP	Ron Davis
MGR	Tom Kelly

WHITE SOX

C	Ray Schalk
1B	Frank Thomas
2B	Nellie Fox
SS	Luke Appling
3B	Bill Melton
OF	Minnie Minoso
OF	Joe Jackson
OF	Harold Baines
SP	Ted Lyons
RP	Hoyt Wilhelm
MGR	Al Lopez

YANKEES

C	Yogi Berra
1B	Lou Gehrig
2B	Tony Lazzeri
SS	Phil Rizzuto
3B	Red Rolfe
OF	Babe Ruth
OF	Joe DiMaggio
OF	Mickey Mantle
SP	Whitey Ford
RP	Goose Gossage
MGR	Casey Stengel

LIKE NO OTHER SPORT

An appreciation of baseball does not come easily. Unlike football, a spectacle that can instantly spark almost anyone's interest, baseball requires its fans to come out to the park equipped with a solid grounding in the fundamentals of the game . . . not only a knowledge of rules . . . but also an understanding of baseball's reliance on records and statistics, a sense of the sport's history.

—Damon Rice
Seasons Past (1976)

Every other sport is held in by boundaries, some of absolute set size, some not; football, hockey, tennis, basketball, golf. But there's no limit to the size of a baseball field. What other sport can claim that? And there's no more enigmatic game; I don't have to tell you that.

—W.P. Kinsella
The Iowa Baseball Confederacy (1986)

Baseball is green and safe. It has neither the street intimidation of basketball nor the controlled Armageddon of football. . . . Baseball is a green dream that happens on summer nights in safe places in unsafe cities.

—Luke Salisbury
The Answer Is Baseball *(1989)*

I prefer baseball, I think, because it's a game of strict accountability. It's much more like the American system than football. If somebody screws up, you know who it is, you don't have to look at the films.

—Edward Bennett Williams
Orioles owner (1983–88)

This ain't football. We do this every day.

—Earl Weaver
Orioles manager (1968–82, '85–86)

Baseball has no penalties at all. A home run is a home run. You cheer. In football, on a score, you look for flags. If there's one, who's it on? When can we cheer? Football acts can be repealed. Baseball acts stand forever.

—Thomas Boswell
The Heart of the Order *(1989)*

The game isn't played by three-hundred-pound steroid gulpers, like football, or seven-foot pituitary freaks, like basketball. Baseball players, when you see them in person, are surprisingly regular-looking guys and must rely on their wits.

—*Dan Gutman*
It Ain't Cheating if You Don't Get Caught (1990)

Baseball is the only game in America for normal people. To play basketball, you have to be seven-feet-six. To play football, you have to have the same width.

—*Bill Veeck (1914–86)*
baseball executive

Ballplayers have a sense of history like no other athletes, if only because baseball *has* a history . . . . A football player has nothing to measure himself against because his game is constantly changing and obliterating its past, so that if they asked one how he could defend against, say Ernie Nevers or Steve Van Buren, he'd probably wonder who the devil you were talking about, and why.

—*Wilfrid Sheed*
Baseball and Lesser Sports (1991)

Baseball mystique calls for brandishing confidences. Everyone starts out expecting great things. In football, by contrast, the prevailing approach to every game is carefully stimulated apprehension.

—*Leonard Koppett*
The New Thinking Fan's Guide to Baseball *(1991)*

Baseball happens to be a game of cumulate tension . . . . football, basketball and hockey are played with hand grenades and machine guns.

—*John Leonard*
New York Times *(1975)*

Baseball and football are very different games. In a way, both of them are easy. Football is easy if you're crazy as hell. Baseball is easy if you've got patience. They'd both be easier for me if I were a little more crazy — and a little more patient.

—*Bo Jackson*
Royals outfielder (1986–90)
Raiders running back (1987–90)

Football strategy is constantly evolving. The last baseball manager to make an original move was Zack Taylor in 1951. He sent a midget to bat for the St. Louis Browns.

—Dan Daly and Bob O'Donnell
The Pro Football Chronicle *(1990)*

When he didn't have time, a few seconds in which to think, it was different. That was why he was better in football and basketball than he was in baseball. In football and basketball, you didn't have time to think as you did in baseball. That made the difference.

—James T. Farrell
Fathers and Sons *(1940)*

You'll see NFL wide receivers make catches like the one Willie Mays made in the '54 World Series several times a season. And Mays didn't have [defensive backs] Ronnie Lott and Jack Tatum to worry about. He also had a glove.

—Dan Daly and Bob O'Donnell
The Pro Football Chronicle *(1990)*

We're not football. We're not basketball. We're baseball and we're different . . . . Why do we have to have a frenetic pace all the time? To people who don't know the game and can't appreciate the nuances, at times the game seems slow. Slowness and casualness *are* baseball.

—Joe Brown
Pirates executive (1955–   )

Hockey is my kind of sport. You can get your feelings out on the ice. Baseball is you and the pitcher. Strike out and you gotta go back to the dugout and wait until the next time up . . . I can't stand those feelings inside me. That's the trouble with ball. There's no outlet in the game.

—Richie Hebner
Pirates infielder (1968–76, '82–83)

I can't stand to watch a baseball game. There is just no action. It's dull. I do enjoy playing baseball, but I'd rather watch basketball or hockey.

—Jim Lonborg
Red Sox pitcher (1965–71)

Pitching is seventy-five per cent of the game, and that's why it's so dull. How many times have you seen a fan napping in the middle of a football or basketball game? Hell, in baseball, people nap all the time.

—Charles O. Finley
Athletics owner (1961–80)

For vivacity, I would compare baseball with chess or billiards. It is somewhat less exciting than a spelling bee.

—Louis Graves
writer (1916)

Baseball is dull only to dull minds.

—Red Smith (1906–82)
sportswriter

The larger the ball, the less the writing about the sport. There are superb books about golf, very good books about baseball, not many good books about football, and very few good books about basketball. There are no books about beachballs.

—George Plimpton (b. 1927)
author

In baseball you hit a home run over the right field fence, the left field fence, the centerfield fence. Nobody cares. In golf, everything has got to be right over second base.

—Ken Harrelson (b. 1941)
White Sox broadcaster

Baseball players ought to try playing golf for a living. No guarantees, all expenses paid — by yourself. I'd like to hear them complain then.

—Al Geiberger (b. 1937)
pro golfer

I don't want to play golf. When I hit a ball, I want someone else to go chase it.

—Rogers Hornsby
Cardinals infielder (1915–26)

The other sports are just sports. Baseball is a love.

—Bryant Gumbel (b. 1948)
broadcaster

THEN AND NOW

I believe in the Rip van Winkle theory — that a man from 1910 must be able to wake up after being asleep for seventy years, walk into a ballpark and understand baseball perfectly.

—Bowie Kuhn
Commissioner of Baseball (1969–84)

Baseball is the only thing besides the paper clip that hasn't changed.

—Bill Veeck (1914–86)
baseball executive

Changes . . . have been profound and lasting. Others have been cosmetic, but today the under-forty fans wouldn't know baseball without them — exploding scoreboards, names on your back, numbers on your front, gloves when you're at bat as well as in the field, and baseball not just under the lights but under roofs too, on artificial grass.

— Bob Feller
Indians pitcher (1936–41, '45–56)

Baseball is different today. They got a lot of kids now whose uniforms are so tight, especially the pants, that they cannot bend over to pick up ground balls. And they don't want to bend over on television games because in that way there's no way their face can get on the camera.

—Casey Stengel
Mets manager (1962–65)

The only kind of spirit you see today in baseball is the kind you drink.

—Johnny Mize
Cardinals first baseman (1936–41)

Every day in every way, baseball gets fancier. A few more years and they'll be playing on oriental rugs.

—*Russell Baker (b. 1925)*
The New York Times *columnist*

Nowadays, they have more trouble packing hair dryers than baseball equipment.

—*Bob Feller*
Indians pitcher (1936–41, '45–56)

Today, players receive pats on the back. There's really no other way to handle people armed with long-term, guaranteed contracts.

—*Roger Craig*
Giants manager (1985–92)

Look at the contrast in salaries between today and my day. I wish my mama had better timing.

—*Monte Irvin*
Giants outfielder (1949–55)

To the modern-day player, a foreign country is Cleveland. A foreign phrase is "My turn to buy" . . . culture is a portable compact disc player. History is a box score.

—Dick Williams
No More Mister Nice Guy *(1990)*

Today's baseball players are walking conglomerates. They have fantastic salaries, multiple investments . . . but we had one thing they don't have today — the train ride. We didn't always like it, but those rides kept us close as a team and as friends, something you can't get on a two-hour plane ride that used to take you fifteen hours on a train.

—Duke Snider
Dodgers outfielder (1947–62)

Today, everybody gets along because so many have the same agent. . . . Everybody goes out to dinner with friends on the other team. So players don't hate each other as much as players used to.

—Frank White
Royals second baseman (1973–90)

My high salary for one season was forty-six thousand dollars and a Cadillac. If I were to get paid a million, I'd feel that I should sweep out the stadium every night after I finished playing the game.

—*Duke Snider*
Dodgers outfielder (1947–62)

There are a lot more college guys in the game today. There has to be since the minor leagues are folding. But the players aren't any smarter.

—*Ernie Lombardi*
Reds catcher (1932–41)

Kids don't learn the fundamentals of baseball at the games any more. You should enter the ballpark the way you enter a church.

—*Bill Lee*
Red Sox pitcher (1969–78)

Today pretty near anybody in the lineup can hit the ball out of the park. In my day, before they started feeding the baseball Wheaties, you had two or three fellows who could do that, and that was all.

—*Roger Peckinpaugh*
Yankees infielder (1913–21)

I have heard of managers who encourage players not to slide hard for fear they will get hurt and be lost from the lineup for a time. That is why you occasionally see a player go into second base on a double-play ball and not even bother to slide. I wonder: could Ty Cobb sit through plays like that and hold his lunch?

—Frank Robinson
Orioles manager (1988–91)

I think the hitter has the advantage today, simply because the pitchers aren't allowed to throw at them in any way. And that takes the edge from the pitcher . . . . Back in my day, if the guy in front of me hit a home run, I went down. It was automatic. You expected it.

—Roy Sievers
Senators first baseman (1954–59)

Every rule change over the past ten years has been against pitchers: lowering the mound, the designated hitter . . . . I've got a kid six years old. He likes sports, but I definitely won't let him pitch. There would be too many things against him.

—Gaylord Perry
Indians pitcher (1972–75)

Probably the most dramatic change in pitching I've observed in my years in baseball has been the disappearance of the knockdown or brushback pitch . . . this is why record numbers of home runs are flying out of ballparks, why earned-run averages are soaring, and why there are so few twenty-game winners in the majors.

—Frank Robinson
Orioles manager (1988–91)

Now you get the manager outraging traditionalists like myself when he signs a pitcher and says, "I hope you can give me five good innings." If you pitched only five good innings in the old days you were a bum.

—Shirley Povich (b. 1905)
Washington Post *sportswriter*

The difference between relief pitching when I did it and today is simple: there's too much of it. It's one of those cases where more is not necessarily better.

—Bob Feller
Indians pitcher (1936–41, '45–56)

Cardinals pitcher Dizzy Dean completed more than sixty per cent of his starts during the 1930s—an unheard of rate for today's relief-dependent pitchers.

Most of the guys that you talk to can remember almost every game that they ever played in because they loved it, and it was in their hearts. . . . I guess there are some players today who feel that way, but I don't think there are enough of them. We really enjoyed it — we treasured every moment.

—Monte Irvin
Giants outfielder (1949–55)

The past is nice. I enjoyed my playing days and the memories are priceless. But you must live in the present.

—Tommy Bridges
Tigers pitcher (1930–43, '45–46)

People who live in the past generally are afraid to compete in the present . . . . I've got my faults, but living in the past isn't one of them. There's no future in it.

—Sparky Anderson
Tigers manager (1979–)

I think one of the most difficult things for anyone who's played baseball is to accept the fact that maybe the players today are playing just as well as ever.

—Ralph Kiner
Pirates outfielder (1946–53)

Nostalgia is a dangerous obsession. It turns stumblebums into princes and dunghills into shining mountain peaks. It makes yesterday sweeter than tomorrow can ever be.

—David Lamb
Stolen Season (1991)

I think history and tradition are very important. But it's not the most important thing for (young players) at this age. It's where they're gonna go, what they're gonna do. *They* want to make some history too.

—Syd Thrift
The Game According to Syd (1990)

I remember the smell of fresh grass and the sun and the clean air. Now my boy comes down to the field and we have artificial turf and lights at night. You mostly smell stale hot dogs and phony grass, but the idea of baseball is still there. Baseball is an inheritance that's passed down from generation to generation.

—Nelson Briles
Pirates pitcher (1971–73)

I stand on the pitcher's mound, the batter at home plate. We are surrounded by every manifestation of civilization: the manicured field, the rising grandstand, the railway beyond the outfield, the buildings on the bluff. Yet my action in throwing and his in swinging are echoes of the most primitive brutality.

—*Eric Rolfe Greenberg*
The Celebrant *(1983)*

OCTOBER'S GAME

Baseball is really two sports — the summer game and the autumn game. One is the leisurely pastime of our national mythology. The other is not so gentle.

—Thomas Boswell
How Life Imitates the World Series (1982)

The playoffs are the wedge between the season and the World Series. If you lose, it means you won't be going to the greatest sports event in this country. It's the quagmire before the promised land. It's the Red Sea that has to be crossed. If you don't cross into the World Series, you're a loser. You're forgotten by Thanksgiving.

—Tim McCarver
Oh Baby, I Love It! (1987)

The playoffs were so exciting, you stood there getting goose bumps before the games began. You throw everything out then and say, "I have to do this now *in here*, not out there." Oh, God, I love it!

—*Rick Sutcliffe*
Cubs pitcher (1984–91)

If you played in a World Series, people get the impression that you were somewhat more of an outstanding player than if you never did. You're put in a kind of special category if you were on a pennant-winning team.

—*Ned Garver*
Browns pitcher (1948–52)

The World Series is American sport's annual ticket to a romantic yesterday, when we were all young and surely going to be in the big leagues someday.

—*Ray Fitzgerald*
The Sporting News *(1981)*

The World Series is best read as a convergence of franchises, an interlocking of fortunate fates, a simultaneous cresting of two waves straining to reach a final shore.

—John Krich
"Blues for a Lost October" (1989)

The Fall Classic has become a metaphor for America's love with baseball . . . for a few golden days every October, each of us becomes a self-anointed expert. . . . the Fall Classic evokes a continuum of memories. We mark chapters in our lives by the World Series we recall.

—George Bush (b. 1924)
40th President of the United States

The gods decree a heavyweight title match only once in a while and a national election only every four years, but there is a World Series with every revolution of the earth around the sun.

—Jacques Barzun
"God's Country and Mine" (1954)

Unlike most championship events, the World Series remains largely free of pageantry, sporting only the traditional tricolor bunting on the facade of each ballpark deck. It needs nothing more; the event is majestic enough.

—Paul Adomites
October's Game (1990)

Many of us can no more remember our first World Series exposure than our first hot dog or first haircut. That is because it is an experience woven and rewoven into so much of our existence.

—Edwin Pope
"Mark Twain's World Series" (1985)

Wherever civilization reigned, and in Jersey City, one question alone was on every lip: who would win? Octogenarians mumbled it. Infants lisped it. Tired businessmen, trampled underfoot in the rush for the West Farms express, asked it of the ambulance attendants who carried them to the hospital.

—P.G. Wodehouse
The Pitcher and the Plutocrat (1910)

The opener of the World Series is different. There is nothing tentative about it; something invariably is proved by it. The speed of a team is established, the strength or weaknesses of its outfielders' throwing arms, the depth of its bench, and the way the tide of luck is running, all these manifest themselves in the first game between rivals not used to playing each other.

—*Arnold Hano*
A Day in the Bleachers (1955)

It's the same as any other ballgame you'll remember as long as you live.

—*Joe Garagiola*
Cardinals catcher (1946–51)

I don't know what it is. The big crowds. The hundreds of reporters, photographers and television men. The flags decorating the stadium. The thought of all that money involved. The presence of celebrities. Whatever it is, you suddenly feel the excitement of it all and nothing that happened before is important.

—*Bob Gibson*
Cardinals pitcher (1959–75)

Do you know that I was scared to death every time I went into a World Series? Every single one, even after I'd been in so many. It's a terrific strain. But once I'd fielded the first ball, it was just another ballgame. Well, almost.

—*Heinie Groh*
Giants infielder (1912–13, '22–26)

I was too excited about being in a World Series and winning, so I relaxed and sang hymns to myself.

—*Orel Hershiser*
Dodgers pitcher (1983–   )

They say the first World Series is the one you remember most. No, no, no! I guarantee you don't remember that one because that fantasy world you always dreamed about is suddenly real. And the thing has ten thousand legs and it simply eats you up.

—*Sparky Anderson*
Reds manager (1970–78)

The only reason I don't like playing in the World Series is I can't watch myself play.

—*Reggie Jackson*
Yankees outfielder (1977–81)

Pitchers start out the World Series with a built-in advantage; many of the batters they face have never hit against them before . . . but the grace period for pitchers is short, and the names of the Series' greatest performers tend to be the same as those in Cooperstown.

—Paul Adomites
October's Game *(1990)*

There is no rhyme or reason for whom the October moment will bless. Such is the beauty of the event itself, however, that while we might not be able to predict a World Series hero, there has nary been one to have faded from memory.

—Bill Madden
The Sporting News *(1980)*

It is an occasion replete with opportunity; for seven games or less, all men are created equal. In World Series history the names of Wambsganss, Larsen and Amoros loom larger than those of Cobb, Hornsby and Williams.

—Donald Honig
The World Series (1986)

My idea of conceit would be a political speaker that would go on the air when the World Series is on.

—*Will Rogers (1879–1935)*
humorist

No presidential campaign can seriously begin until after the World Series.

—*John F. Kennedy (1917–63)*
35th President of the United States

THE FIVE BIGGEST
WORLD SERIES UPSETS

1914: BOSTON BRAVES
BEAT PHILADELPHIA ATHLETICS

In mid-July the woeful Braves were mired in last place of the National League. They then staged a dramatic turn-around to win the pennant in September. Still, no one expected them to beat the powerful A's, who clinched their fourth pennant in five years on the strength of its "Million Dollar Infield" and three future Hall-of-Fame pitchers (Charles "Chief" Bender, Herb Pennock, and Eddie Plank). Shockingly, outmanned Boston not only beat Philadelphia, but did so with a decisive four-game sweep. Henceforth, they would be known as "The Miracle Braves."

1926: ST. LOUIS CARDINALS
BEAT NEW YORK YANKEES

The Cardinals clawed their way to a pennant for the first time in thirty-eight years, only to face the formidable Yankee "Murderer's Row" (Babe Ruth, Lou Gehrig, Bob Meusel, Earl Combs, and Tony Lazzeri), who were one year away from producing the greatest single season of any team ever. Despite the apparent mismatch, St. Louis split the first six games, then won the deciding contest when an aging and badly hung-over Grover Cleveland Alexander came out of the bullpen in the late innings, halting a rally by striking out Tony Lazzeri. In the ninth, the Yankees self-destructed when tying run Babe Ruth was caught stealing, ending the game and giving the Redbirds a surprising World Championship.

1954: NEW YORK GIANTS
BEAT CLEVELAND INDIANS

Boasting one of the greatest pitching staffs ever assembled, the Indians breezed to the American League title with a record 111 victories, making them heavy favorites over a good-but-not-great Giants team. A sensational over-the-shoulder grab by New York outfielder Willie Mays in Game One — the most famous catch in Series history — shifted the momentum to New York. The Tribe was swept in four straight and has never recovered. Since that time, no Cleveland team has come close to winning a division or a pennant — let alone a World Series.

1969: NEW YORK METS
BEAT BALTIMORE ORIOLES

Until 1969, the Mets were a comedy monologue staple, a team synonymous with failure. In fact, '69 was the first winning season in franchise history. Small wonder, then, that the Mets were pegged as underdogs against the Orioles, who won their pennant race by 19 games. Baltimore breezed to an easy win in the opening game, but then the Mets won the next four, thanks to great pitching, spectacular circus catches, tape-measure home runs from weak hitters, and at least two surreal rulings by the umpires. In a year when Americans witnessed the first man on the moon, the Amazing Mets as World Series champions seemed only slightly less miraculous.

1988: LOS ANGELES DODGERS
BEAT OAKLAND ATHLETICS

After languishing among the also-rans the year before, the Dodgers rebounded to win the National League pennant. But they seemed ill-equipped to topple the star-laden

Athletics, who boasted baseball's best home run hitter, base-stealer, and relief pitcher. Crippling injuries had so badly weakened L.A. that the Dodgers lineup more closely resembled that of its Albuquerque farm team. Despite the apparent mismatch, the Dodgers won the opener when a limping Kirk Gibson hobbled off the bench to smash a game-winning pinch-hit home run in the bottom of the ninth. The blow deflated the mighty A's, who fell quietly in five games.

DIAMOND TWILIGHT

When you first sign that contract as a kid, they tell you your whole future is ahead of you. But they forget to tell you that your future stops at thirty-five.

—Hal Jeffcoat
Reds pitcher (1956–59)

It's a mere moment in a man's life between the all-star game and an old-timer's game.

—Vin Scully (b. 1927)
Dodgers broadcaster

Why am I wasting so much dedication on a mediocre career?

—Ron Swoboda
Mets outfielder (1965–70)

It's that I can't see the ball the way I used to. It used to come floating up with all seven continents showing, and the pitcher's thumbprint, and a grass smooch or two, and the Spalding guarantee and the ten-point sans-serif, and whop! I could feel the sweet wood with the bat still cocked. Now, there's a cloud around it, a sort of spiral vagueness . . . .

—*John Updike*
The Slump *(1968)*

Your body is just like a bar of soap. It gradually wears down from repeated use.

—*Dick Allen*
Athletics first baseman (1977)

You start chasing a ball and your brain immediately commands your body to "Run forward! Bend! Scoop up the ball! Peg it to the infield!" Then your body says, "Who, me?"

—*Joe DiMaggio*
Yankees outfielder (1936–42, '46–51)

He threw it in a spot where I used to be a good hitter.

—*Bob Boone*
Royals catcher (1989–90)

I'm throwing twice as hard as I ever did. It's just not getting there as fast.

—*Lefty Gomez*
Yankees pitcher (1930–43)

Young horse runs fast, old horse knows the way.

—*Bill North*
Giants outfielder (1979–81)

Age is a question of mind over matter. If you don't mind, age don't matter.

—*Satchel Paige*
Browns pitcher (1951–53)

When you get to be my age, you don't hold out, you hold on.

—*Walker Cooper*
Braves catcher (1953)

I knew when it was over. I'd look at the on-deck circle and see two rookies fighting over who was going to get to hit against me.

—*Sparky Lyle*
White Sox pitcher (1982)

People like us are afraid to leave ball. What else is there to do? . . . . When baseball has been your whole life, you can't think about a future without it, so you hang on as long as you can . . . you've got to prove to yourself beyond a doubt that you can't play anymore. If your teammates and the fans find it sad, at least you can say to yourself, "I'm through." So what if everybody else decided that long before?

—*Willie Stargell*
Pirates first baseman (1962–82)

I'd walk through hell in a gasoline suit to keep playing baseball.

—*Pete Rose*
Reds infielder (1963–79, '84–86)

A waiver means that your arm is in the ragbag and the old clothes man is singing his twilight song to the little birdies in the trees.

—Nick Altrock
White Sox pitcher (1903-09)

All ballplayers should quit when it starts to feel as if all the baselines run uphill.

—Babe Ruth
Yankees outfielder (1920–34)

I put my whole heart and soul into baseball. Then, one day, it was all over. When you leave baseball, you leave a part of your childhood behind.

—Sandy Vance
Dodgers pitcher (1970–71)

I loved the game. I loved the competition. But I never had any fun. I never enjoyed it. All hard work, all the time.

—Carl Yastrzemski
Red Sox outfielder (1961–83)

They told me my services were no longer desired because they wanted to put in a youth program as an advance way of keeping the club going. I'll never make the mistake of being seventy years old again.

—Casey Stengel
Yankees manager (1949–60)

I have a great many friends in baseball, but the day I hung up my uniform, I never saw so many doors close so quickly. My phone stopped ringing and I didn't hear from anybody.

—Don Hoak
Phillies third baseman (1963–64)

I never felt as bad when my father died as I did when I was released by the Cardinals.

—Enos Slaughter
Cardinals outfielder (1938–42, '46–53)

When you shut the door on baseball, you have to keep it closed or it will never let you go.

—Dick Bosman
Athletics pitcher (1975–76)

It seems that ballplayers' lives attain some sort of dumb resonance only after accumulating the dust of time. We depend on yellowing newsprint and record books to tell us who we are.

—Tom Grimes
Season's End (1992)

When my playing days were over I couldn't go to a ballgame. I still can't. Maybe inside there's a feeling that I can do better than the guys out there . . . . now I'm on the other side of the fence, they've locked me out, and it's cold.

—Gene Conley
Red Sox pitcher (1961–63)

As a major league player you never even touch your luggage — never even have to make a decision for yourself if you don't want to. . . . A lot of ballplayers in the big leagues when I played just weren't prepared for the real world . . . because when you get home the fear sets in that all of a sudden you haven't got anybody to take care of you anymore.

—Dick Ellsworth
Brewers pitcher (1970–71)

It's an unreal life, and when you leave it, you're lost. You can't deal with reality. They keep pushing money at you and then one day they suddenly stop and you find yourself standing in an unemployment line, hiding your face so former friends won't see you.

—John Roseboro
Glory Days with the Dodgers *(1978)*

When I was hitting home runs in the sandlot in Brooklyn somewhere, nobody would have called me to MGM. But that's how I made the transition. Thank goodness the Cubs had a [minor] league team in L.A. If I had been playing in Boston, they'd have sent me to Louisville and they don't make movies in Louisville.

—Chuck Connors
actor/Cubs first baseman (1951)

I threw a baseball for twenty years. What do I know about running any kind of business?

—Bobby Shantz
Phillies pitcher (1964)

He missed the sensation of the sock — the moment the stomach galloped just before the wood hit the ball, and the satisfying sting that sped through his arms and shoulders as he belted one . . . he missed the special exercise of running the bases, whirling 'round them with the speed of a racehorse as nine frantic men tried to cut him down.

—*Bernard Malamud*
The Natural *(1952)*

I know I find myself a helluva lot better ballplayer since I quit playing.

—*Joe Garagiola (b. 1926)*
broadcaster

Fifty years from now I'll be just three inches of type in a record book.

—*Brooks Robinson*
Orioles third baseman (1955–77)

THE FIVE SADDEST DAYS
IN BASEBALL

August 16, 1920: Cleveland Indians shortstop Ray Chapman is hit in the head by a submarine pitch from Yankee Carl Mays. After taking two steps toward first base, Chapman collapses and is carried from the field. He dies the next day of a fractured skull. Chapman was 29 years old. To this day, he remains the only player ever to be killed in a major league baseball game.

September 28, 1920: An Illinois grand jury indicts eight members of the Chicago White Sox for conspiring to throw the 1919 World Series, a series the heavily favored

Sox lost to the underdog Cincinnati Reds. Less than a year later, all eight are banned from baseball for life, despite being cleared in a Chicago court. Among those exiled from the game is Joe Jackson, whose .356 lifetime batting average is the second highest in history.

July 4, 1939: Before 61,808 fans at sold-out Yankee Stadium, Lou Gehrig chokes back tears as he gives his farewell speech. The "Iron Horse," the most durable player baseball has ever known, is dying from amyotrophic lateral sclerosis (later to be known as Lou Gehrig's Disease). Despite his tragic fate, Gehrig claims to the crowd, "Today, I consider myself the luckiest man on the face of the earth."

June 12, 1981: After several months of bitter labor disputes, the Major League Players Association announces it will go on strike against the owners, and no further games will be played until the issues are resolved. The work stoppage lasts for 50 days, the longest sports strike in American history. The strike ends on July 31. Nearly forty per cent of the season—706 games in all—is lost.

October 17, 1989: Just minutes before the third game of the World Series between the Oakland Athletics and San

Yankee Stadium, July 4, 1939: Lou Gehrig says
goodbye to baseball.

Francisco Giants is scheduled to start, a major earthquake rips through the Bay Area. The quake causes structural damage to Candlestick Park and more than a billion dollars of devastation throughout the region. Sixty-four residents are killed and thousands are left homeless. The Series is delayed a record ten days before resuming; the A's sweep the Giants in four straight games.

LEGENDS OF COOPERSTOWN

The strongest thing baseball has going for it today is yester-days.

—*Lawrence Ritter*
The Glory of Their Times (1966)

HENRY AARON

I looked for the same pitch my whole career. A breaking ball. All the time. I never worried about the fastball. They couldn't throw it past me. None of 'em.

—*Henry Aaron*
Braves outfielder (1954–74)

Henry Aaron is simply smarter than all the pitchers. He deceives pitchers. One of his secrets is his slow manner. He puts pitchers to sleep.

—*Ernie Johnson*
Braves broadcaster (1966–90)

Aaron's excellence was not expelled in blinding bursts of energy but rather played out, patiently and inexorably, over a whole generation.

—*Lonnie Wheeler*
I Had a Hammer (1991)

Trying to throw a fastball by Hank Aaron is like trying to sneak the sunrise past a rooster.

—*Curt Simmons*
Phillies pitcher (1947–50, '52–60)

More than anyone else, he's made me wish I wasn't a manager.

—*Walter Alston*
Dodgers manager (1954–76)

ERNIE BANKS

Awards mean a lot, but they don't say it all. The people in baseball mean more to me than statistics.

—Ernie Banks
Cubs infielder (1953–71)

Ernie rejoices merely in living and baseball is a marvelous extra that makes his existence so much more pleasurable.

—Arthur Daley
"Report on Life in the Geriatric Set" (1971)

His wrists are the secret of Banks' success. Instead of taking the big, Ruthian-type swing of the lively ball era, he swings his bat as if it were a buggy whip, striking at the ball with the reflexive swiftness of a serpent's tongue.

—Bill Furlong
Baseball Stars of 1959

He never complained about his team's bad luck or bad talent, never stopped playing the game with joy, never stopped giving his all, never lost his proud demeanor, and never acted like anything but a winner. He was a symbol of the Cub fan's undiminishing resilience. If he could be happy to come to the park each afternoon, then so could we.

—Joe Mantegna (b. 1947)
actor

JOHNNY BENCH

I can throw out any man alive.

—Johnny Bench
Reds catcher (1967–83)

Every time Bench throws, everybody in baseball drools.

—Harry Dalton
Orioles general manager (1965–1971)

I don't want to embarrass any other catcher by comparing him with Johnny Bench.

—*Sparky Anderson*
Reds manager (1970–78)

He'll come out on the mound and treat me like a two-year-old, but so help me, I like it.

— *Jim Maloney*
Reds pitcher (1960–70)

YOGI BERRA

So I'm ugly. So what? I don't hit with my face.

—*Yogi Berra*
Yankees catcher (1947–63)

Yogi had the fastest bat I ever saw. He could hit a ball late — that was already past him — and take it out of the park. The pitchers were afraid of him 'cause he'd hit anything . . . so they didn't know what to throw to him. Yogi had 'em psyched out and he wasn't even trying to psych 'em out.

—*Hector Lopez*
Yankees outfielder (1959–66)

He seemed to be doing everything wrong, yet everything came out right. He stopped everything behind the plate and hit everything in front of it.

—Mel Ott
Giants manager (1942–48)

While he did mangle a phrase now and then, with Yogi it was important that you listen to what he was saying, not how; and what he said generally made very good sense.

—Donald Honig
The New York Mets (1986)

They say he's funny. Well, he has a lovely wife and family, a beautiful home, money in the bank, and he plays golf with millionaires. What's funny about that?

—Casey Stengel
Yankees manager (1949–60)

ROD CAREW

There is a special sensation in getting good wood on the ball and driving a double down the left-field line as the crowd in the ballpark rises to its feet and cheers. But I also remember how much fun I had as a skinny barefoot kid hitting a tennis ball with a broomstick on a quiet, dusty street in Panama.

—Rod Carew
Twins infielder (1967–78)

There are a number of guys who know how to steal as well as Rod. But there's nobody alive who can turn a single into a double or a double into a triple the way Rod can.

—Frank Quilici
Twins manager (1972–75)

He's the only guy I know who can go four-for-three.

—Alan Bannister
White Sox infielder (1976–80)

TY COBB

I had to fight all my life to survive. They were all against me . . . but I beat the bastards and left them in the ditch.

—*Ty Cobb*
Tigers outfielder (1905–26)

Cobb is a prick. But he sure can hit. God Almighty, that man can hit.

—*Babe Ruth*
Yankees outfielder (1920–34)

The Babe was a great ballplayer, sure. But Cobb was even greater. Babe could knock your brains out, but Cobb would drive you crazy.

—*Tris Speaker*
Indians outfielder (1916–26)

He was the strangest of all our national sports idols. But not even his disagreeable character could destroy the image of his greatness as a ballplayer. Ty Cobb was the best. That seemed to be all he wanted.

—*Jimmy Cannon (1910–73)*
sportswriter

Let him sleep if he will. If you get him riled up, he will annihilate us.

—**Connie Mack**
Athletics manager (1901–50)

He was still fighting the Civil War, and as far as he was concerned, we were all damn Yankees. But who knows, if he hadn't had that terrible persecution complex, he never would've been about the best ballplayer who ever lived.

—**Sam Crawford**
Tigers outfielder (1903–17)

Cobb lived off the field as though he wished to live forever. He lived on the field as though it was his last day.

—**Branch Rickey**
Browns manager (1913–15)

ROBERTO CLEMENTE

I would be lost without baseball. I don't think I could stand being away from it as long as I was alive.

—*Roberto Clemente*
Pirates outfielder (1955–72)

He looked like he was falling apart when he ran. Looked like he was coming apart when he threw. His stance at the plate was ridiculous . . . he really looked less like a ballplayer than anyone I'd ever seen. It was a crazy thing. The only thing that made him look sensational was the results.

—*Robin Roberts*
Phillies pitcher (1948–61)

He played the kind of baseball that none of us had ever seen before — throwing and running and hitting at something close to the level of absolute perfection, playing to win but also playing the game almost as if it were a form of punishment for everyone else on the field.

—*Roger Angell*
Five Seasons (1971)

DIZZY DEAN

Anybody who's ever had the privilege of seein' me play knows that I am the greatest pitcher in the world.

—Jay Hanna "Dizzy" Dean
Cardinals pitcher (1930–37)

Yes — it's Dean, Dean, Dean — he's a beggar with a bullet through your spleen . . . though at times some bat has flayed you, by the Texas sun that made you . . . you're a better man than bats are, Dizzy Dean.

—Grantland Rice
New York Sun *(1934)*

When ole Diz was out there pitching it was more than just another ballgame. It was a regular three-ring circus and everybody was wide awake and enjoying being alive.

—Pepper Martin
Cardinals outfielder (1928–40, '44)

JOE DIMAGGIO

I'd like to thank the good Lord for making me a Yankee.

—Joe DiMaggio
Yankees outfielder (1936–42, '46–51)

You saw him standing out there and you knew you had a pretty damn good chance to win the baseball game.

—Red Ruffing
Yankees pitcher (1930–42, '45–46)

Joe DiMaggio batting sometimes gave the impression . . . the suggestion that the old rules and dimensions of baseball no longer applied to him, and that the game had at last grown unfairly easy.

—Donald Hall
Fathers Playing Catch with Sons *(1985)*

He had the greatest instinct of any ballplayer I ever saw. He made the rest of them look like plumbers.

—Art Passarella
American League umpire (1941–42, '45–53)

"I would like to take the great DiMaggio fishing," the old man said. "They say his father was a fisherman. Maybe he was as poor as we are and would understand."

—Ernest Hemingway
The Old Man and the Sea (1952)

DON DRYSDALE

I hate all hitters. I start a game mad and I stay that way until it's over. I guess I'm a perfectionist. When I throw a curve that hangs, and it goes for a hit, I want to chew up my glove.

—Don Drysdale
Dodgers pitcher (1956–69)

The trick against Drysdale is to hit him before he hits you.

—Orlando Cepeda
Giants first baseman (1958–66)

Don Drysdale would consider an intentional walk a waste of three pitches. If he wants to put you on base, he can hit you with one.

—*Mike Shannon*
Cardinals third baseman (1962–70)

Batting against Don Drysdale is the same as making a date with the dentist.

—*Dick Groat*
Pirates shortstop (1952, '55–62)

JIMMIE FOXX

Let me get a good grip on that bat, as if I wanted to leave my fingerprints on the wood: let me swing with a quick snap which comes from a powerful wrist, and, if I've gotten back of the ball, it sure will travel.

—*Jimmie Foxx*
Athletics first baseman (1925–35)

He has muscles in his hair.

—*Lefty Gomez*
Yankees pitcher (1930–43)

You say you've heard stories about Jimmie's long-distance hitting? Well, I don't know which stories in particular you've heard, but I'd say you wouldn't go far wrong if you believed them all.

—Ted Lyons
White Sox pitcher (1923–46)

When Neil Armstrong first set foot on the moon, he and all the space scientists were puzzled by an unidentifiable white object. I knew immediately what it was. That was a home run ball hit off me in 1937 by Jimmie Fox.

—Lefty Gomez
Yankees pitcher (1930–43)

BOB GIBSON

I guess I was never much in awe of anybody. I think you have to have that attitude if you're going to go far in this game.

—Bob Gibson
Cardinals pitcher (1959–75)

The greatest competitor was Bob Gibson. He worked so fast out there, and he always had the hood up. He always wanted to close his own deal . . . he never talked to you because he was battling so hard. I sure as hell don't miss batting against him, but I miss him in the game.

—*Pete Rose*
Reds infielder (1963–78, '84–86)

Bob Gibson pitches as though he's double-parked.

—*Vin Scully (b. 1927)*
Dodgers broadcaster

Gibson's the luckiest pitcher I've ever seen. Because he always picks the night to pitch when the other team doesn't score any runs.

—*Tim McCarver*
Cardinals catcher (1959–69, '73–74)

WALTER JOHNSON

I throw as hard as I can when I think I have to throw as hard as I can.

—Walter Johnson
Senators pitcher (1907–27)

. . . [his fastball] looked about the size of a watermelon seed and it hissed at you as it passed.

—Ty Cobb
Tigers outfielder (1905–26)

You can't hit what you can't see.

—Ping Bodie
Yankees outfielder (1918–21)

He's got a gun concealed about his person. They can't tell me he throws them balls with his arm.

—Ring Lardner (1885–1933)
sportswriter

Just speed, raw speed, blinding speed, too much speed.

—Ty Cobb
Tigers outfielder (1905–26)

Let there be no more misunderstanding, no delusion, that Walter Johnson is, or was, a baseball legend. Not only inaccurate is that description, it demeans him.

—Shirley Povich (1905-   )
sportswriter

HARMON KILLEBREW

I didn't have evil intentions, but I guess I did have power.

—Harmon Killebrew
Twins infielder (1961–74)

If ever anyone wielded a blunt instrument at home plate, it was Harmon Killebrew. There was nothing subtle about the Idaho strongboy: it was always his intention to mash a pitched ball as hard and as far as he could.

—Donald Honig
The Power Hitters (1989)

He hit line drives that put the opposition in jeopardy. And I don't mean infielders, I mean outfielders.

—Ossie Bluege
Senators farm director (1948–56)

Dodgers strikeout king Sandy Koufax, the dominant
pitcher of the 1960s.

This team without Killebrew is like dressing up for a formal affair with a white tie and tails and then wearing muddy shoes.

—Earl Battey
Twins catcher (1961–67)

Killebrew can knock the ball out of any park, including Yellowstone.

—Paul Richards
Orioles manager (1955–61)

SANDY KOUFAX

A guy who throws what he intends to throw — that's the definition of a good pitcher.

—Sandy Koufax
Dodgers pitcher (1955–66)

Trying to hit him was like trying to drink coffee with a fork.

—Willie Stargell
Pirates first baseman (1962–82)

He throws a "radio ball" — a pitch you hear but you don't see.

—*Gene Mauch*
Phillies manager (1960–68)

He is the greatest Jewish athlete since Samson.

—*George Jessel (1898–1981)*
comedian

MICKEY MANTLE

Sometimes I sit in my den at home and read stories about myself. Kids used to save whole scrapbooks on me. They get tired of 'em and mail 'em to me . . . . I'll go in there and read 'em, and you know what? They might as well be about Musial and DiMaggio. It's like reading about somebody else.

—*Mickey Mantle*
Yankees outfielder (1951–68)

Until I saw Mantle peel down for his shower in the clubhouse at Comiskey Park one afternoon, I never knew how he developed his brutal power, but his bare back looked like a barrelful of snakes.

—Dale Lancaster
Chicago Sun Times (1957)

There is no sound in baseball akin to the sound of Mantle hitting a home run, the crunchy sound of an axe biting into a tree, yet magnified a hundred times in the vast, cavernous, echo-making hollows of a ball field.

—Arnold Hano
Baseball Stars of 1958

Mantle's greatness was built on power and pain. He exuded the first and endured the second, and rarely was there a feature story on him that didn't dwell on both departments.

—Ray Fitzgerald
Boston Globe (1974)

On two legs, Mickey Mantle would have been the greatest ballplayer who ever lived.

—*Nellie Fox*
White Sox second baseman (1950–63)

Sometimes I think if I had the same body and the same natural ability and someone else's brain, who knows how good a player I might have been?

—*Mickey Mantle*
Yankees outfielder (1951–68)

He came out of Oklahoma wearing a straw hat, lugging a four dollar cardboard suitcase. He was that unique specimen, the instant star. He hit the ball longer. He hit it more often, and he hit it from either side of the plate with equal violence. . . . Mickey Mantle. Say the name fast, say it slow; it has a lilt to it. A trick of poetry, that trochaic, alliterative name, but man and name draw the people.

—*Gerald Astor*
Look *(1965)*

WILLIE MAYS

They throw the ball, I hit it. They hit the ball, I catch it.

—Willie Mays
Giants outfielder (1951–72)

Snider, Mantle and Mays — you could get a fat lip in any saloon by starting an argument as to which was best. One point was beyond argument, though. Willie was by all odds the most exciting.

—Red Smith (1906–82)
sportswriter

I'm not sure what the hell charisma is, but I get the feeling it's Willie Mays.

—Ted Kluszewski
Reds first baseman (1947–57)

They invented the All-Star game for Willie Mays.

—Ted Williams
Red Sox outfielder (1939–42, '46–60)

I can't very well tell my batters don't hit it to him. Wherever they hit it, he's there anyway.

—*Gil Hodges*
Mets manager (1968–72)

As a batter, his only weakness is a wild pitch.

—*Bill Rigney*
Giants manager (1956–60)

There have been only two geniuses in the world. Willie Mays and Willie Shakespeare.

—*Tallulah Bankhead (1903–68)*
actress

STAN MUSIAL

The key to hitting for a high average is to relax, concentrate —and don't hit the fly ball to center field.

—*Stan Musial*
Cardinals outfielder (1941–44, '46–63)

He could have hit .300 with a fountain pen.

—Joe Garagiola
Cardinals catcher (1946–51)

Once Musial timed your fastball, your infielders were in jeopardy.

—Warren Spahn
Braves pitcher (1942, '46–64)

I've had pretty good success with Stan — by throwing him my best pitch and backing up third.

—Carl Erskine
Dodgers pitcher (1948–59)

SATCHEL PAIGE

I never threw an illegal pitch. The trouble is, once in a while I toss one that ain't never been seen by this generation.

—Leroy Robert "Satchel" Paige
Negro Leagues pitcher (1926–47, '55)

Satchel Paige was the toughest pitcher I ever faced. I couldn't do much with him. All the years I played there, I never got a hit off him. He threw fire.

—*Buck Leonard*
Negro Leagues first baseman (1933–50)

When Paige wound up to pitch, he looked like a cross between Ichabod Crane and Rip van Winkle.... He was easy to imitate and funny to watch, unless you were the batter trying to hit against him.

—*Al Hirshberg*
Fear Strikes Out (1955)

If Satch and I were pitching on the same team, we'd cinch the pennant by July Fourth and go fishing until World Series time.

—*Dizzy Dean*
Cardinals pitcher (1930–37)

JACKIE ROBINSON

It kills me to lose. If I'm a troublemaker — and I don't think that my temper makes me one — then it's only because I can't stand losing. That's the way I am about winning. All I ever wanted to do was finish first.

—Jackie Robinson
Dodgers infielder (1947–56)

He knew he had to do well. He knew that the future of blacks in baseball depended on it. The pressure was enormous, overwhelming, unbearable at times. I don't know how he held up. I know I never could have.

—Duke Snider
Dodgers outfielder (1947–62)

He was a therapist for the masses by succeeding, by doing it with such style and flair and drama. He helped level baseball off, to make it truly a game for black and white, with excellence the only test for success.

—Reverend Jesse Jackson (b. 1941)
statesman

I remember my father turned to some friends at the store one day and observed, "Well, you can say what you want about that nigger Robinson, but he's got guts."

—*Willie Morris (b. 1934)*
author

Everytime I look at my pocket book, I see Jackie Robinson.

—*Willie Mays*
Giants outfielder (1951–72)

He was the only player I ever saw in a rundown who would be safe more often than out. He ran as if his head was on a swizzle, back and forth, back and forth, until he could get out of it.

—*Bobby Bragan*
Dodgers catcher (1943–44, '47–48)

They call his name in a way no other player's name is called. They plead to shake his hand or ask for his autograph. They touch his clothes as he walks by, unhurrying, pleasant, friendly, cooperative, because Jackie has never lost sight of what the game has meant to him, and what he has meant, means now and will always mean to his people.

—*Milton Gross*
"The Emancipation of Jackie Robinson" (1951)

BABE RUTH

I coulda hit a .400 lifetime average easy. But I woulda had to hit them singles. The people were payin' to see me hit them home runs.

—*Babe Ruth*
Yankees outfielder (1920–34)

It had been a game of "inside baseball," a tightly played contest for single runs — stolen bases, squeeze plays, placement hitting. But the booming bat of the Babe demonstrated that runs could be gathered like bananas — in bunches. He soon had everyone swinging from his heels, shooting for the fences and trying to follow his lead.

—*Arthur Daley*
"Last Out for the Babe" (1948)

No one hit home runs the way Babe did. They were something special. They were like homing pigeons. The ball would leave the bat, pause briefly, suddenly gain its bearings, then take off for the stands.

—*Lefty Gomez*
Yankees pitcher (1930–43)

He had such a beautiful swing, he even looked good striking out.

—*Mark Koenig*
Yankees shortstop (1925–30)

Having seen all the great players of the past four decades, I
will take the word of my elders that Babe Ruth could pitch
and field and throw and run — yes, even run — with the best
of them. And I fully accept that the sum of his ability made him
the most exciting, the most dominant player the game has
ever known.

—*George Vecsey*
New York Times *(1988)*

Some twenty years ago I stopped talking about the Babe for
the simple reason that I realized that those who had never
seen him didn't believe me.

—*Tommy Holmes (1904–75)*
sportswriter

When Babe Ruth died, he took baseball with him. My interest in baseball has passed on, but he never took that aura from me. He always comes back, even today when I hear "play ball!"

—*Samuel Fuller (b. 1911)*
film director

WILLIE STARGELL

Pittsburgh isn't fancy, but it's real . . . it's a working town and money doesn't come easy . . . I feel as much a part of this city as the cobblestone streets and the steel mills . . . people in this town expect an honest day's work, and I've given it to them for a long, long time.

—*Willie Stargell*
Pirates first baseman (1962–82)

Having Willie Stargell on your ballclub is like having a diamond ring on your finger.

—*Chuck Tanner*
Pirates manager (1977–85)

If Willie asked us to jump off the Fort Pitt Bridge, we'd ask him what kind of dive he wanted. That's how much respect we have for the man.

—Al Oliver
Pirates outfielder (1968–77)

He takes it all in stride. It's four shots, a shower and back the next day, even if some of those shots look like they came from Cape Kennedy.

—Richie Hebner
Pirates infielder (1968–76, '82–83)

I never saw anything like it. He doesn't just hit pitchers. He takes away their dignity.

—Don Sutton
Dodgers pitcher (1966–80, '88)

CASEY STENGEL

There comes a time in every man's life, and I've had plenty of them.

—Casey Stengel
Yankees manager (1949–60)

Casey knew his baseball. He only made it look like he was fooling around. . . . He knew every move that was ever invented and some that we haven't even caught on to yet.

—Sparky Anderson
Tigers manager (1979-   )

He doesn't belong in the real world. He belongs in the pages of Grimm's Fairy Tales . . . he's the only man in the world who has his own language, two banks, a golf course, a blue serge suit and non-stop speech.

—Jim Murray
Los Angeles Times *(1971)*

It is fashionable to say that successful people, in any field, could have been whatever they wanted. But you could not picture Casey Stengel being anything else but what he was. The greatest showman baseball ever knew.

—Mickey Herskowitz
Houston Post *(1975)*

HONUS WAGNER

There ain't much to being a ballplayer — if you're a ballplayer.

—*Honus Wagner*
Pirates shortstop (1900–17)

He was the nearest thing to a perfect player no matter where his manager chose to play him.

—*John McGraw*
Giants manager (1902–32)

That goddamned Dutchman is the only man in the game I can't scare.

—*Ty Cobb*
Tigers outfielder (1905–26)

He was very bowlegged, and when he sped from first base to second on one of his seven hundred and twenty stolen bases, he looked like a hoop rolling down the baselines.

—*Fred Lieb*
Baseball as I Have Known It (1977)

There is something Lincolnesque about him, his rugged homeliness, his simplicity, his integrity, and his true nobility of character.

—*Arthur Daley (1904–74)*
sportswriter

He was a gentle, kind man, a storyteller, supportive of rookies, patient with fans, cheerful in hard times, careful of the example he set for youth, a hard worker, a man who had no enemies and who never forgot his friends. He was the most beloved man in baseball before Ruth.

—*Bill James*
The Historical Baseball Abstract (1986)

TED WILLIAMS

A man has to have goals — for a day, for a lifetime — and that was mine, to have people say, "There goes Ted Williams, the greatest hitter who ever lived."

—*Ted Williams*
Red Sox (1939–42, '46–60)

He is a bed of assorted neuroses, as are all artists, from painters to adept street cleaners. . . . he has been over-written, over-publicized — an unconscious victim of a nation's hunger for a superstar to match the frenzied mood of a post-war culture.

—*Bob Considine*
"Spinning Superman" (1946)

Did they tell me how to pitch to Williams? Sure they did. It was great advice, very encouraging. They said he had no weakness, won't swing at a bad ball, has the best eyes in the business, and can kill you with one swing; he won't hit anything bad, but don't give him anything good.

—*Bobby Shantz*
Athletics pitcher (1949–56)

I got a big charge out of seeing Ted Williams hit. Once in a while they let me try to field some of them, which sort of dimmed my enthusiasm.

—*Rocky Bridges*
Senators infielder (1957–58)

Williams is the classic ballplayer of the game on a hot August weekday, before a small crowd, when the only thing at stake is the tissue-thin difference between a thing done well and a thing done ill.

—John Updike
"Hub Fans Bid Kid Adieu" (1960)

FIVE WHO BELONG IN THE HALL OF FAME

RICHIE ASHBURN
Phillies/Cubs/Mets outfielder (1948–62)

Ashburn suffered the misfortune of playing centerfield during the same era as Mays, Mantle, and Snider, who were all better power hitters. Richie also played on only one pennant-winning team. That's it for the negatives. To his credit, Ashburn batted over .300 nine times, won two batting titles, and collected the most hits of any player during the 1950s. The five-time All-Star stole bases in an era where the strategy was uncommon, and was an extraordinary outfielder, leading the league in putouts nine times. Ashburn's curtain call was especially impressive: he was the last man to bat .300 in his final big-league season.

YEARS:	15	HOME RUNS:	29
BATTING AVERAGE:	.308	RUNS BATTED IN:	586
HITS:	2,574	STOLEN BASES:	234
RUNS:	1,322		

GIL HODGES
Dodgers/Mets first baseman (1943, '47–63)

Perhaps the Hall of Fame balloters believe they have already enshrined too many Dodgers from the great Brooklyn teams of the 1950s. But that's no reason to keep Hodges out of Cooperstown. An eight-time All-Star, Hodges drove in 100 or more runs in seven consecutive seasons and hit 20 or more homers for eleven straight years. His lifetime average of .273 is well above that of several other Hall-of-Fame sluggers. Gil was especially brilliant in October, blasting home runs in each of his last four World Series appearances. He was no oaf in the field, either, and won three Gold Gloves. If all this weren't enough, Hodges later became an outstanding manager, guiding the Miracle Mets to the World Championship in 1969.

YEARS:	18	HOME RUNS:	370
BATTING AVERAGE:	.273	RUNS BATTED IN:	1,274
HITS:	1,921	STOLEN BASES:	63
RUNS:	1,105		

JIM KAAT
Senators/Twins/White Sox/Phillies/Yankees/Cardinals pitcher (1959-83)

Only a precious few ballplayers played in four different decades, and Kaat is one of them. His 25 seasons as a big league pitcher was a record until Tommy John broke it in 1989. Kaat won 283 career games, making him the fourth-winningest left-hander in history. Jim won 20 games in three different seasons, while being generally regarded as the greatest fielding pitcher of all time. Only Orioles third baseman Brooks Robinson won as many Gold Gloves as Kaat, and only Kaat and Robinson earned all 16 of theirs consecutively. Such fielding excellence has never been equalled.

YEARS:	25	LOSSES:	237
GAMES:	898	EARNED RUN AVERAGE:	3.45
INNINGS PITCHED:	4,528	COMPLETE GAMES:	180
WINS:	283	STRIKEOUTS:	2,461

BILL MAZEROSKI
Pirates second baseman (1956-72)

Mazeroski is the greatest fielding second baseman of all time, period. End of argument. Even if you never saw his graceful pivot and whip-cracking throws in person, the statistics are there to prove it: eight Gold Gloves as a second baseman, second base major-league records for double plays in a season and a career, eight seasons with the most twin killings, plus eight seasons leading the league in chances and nine in assists. No major-leaguer has equalled any single one of these achievements. Someone who fielded this well could have survived with a weak bat, but Mazeroski was a lifetime .260 hitter with more than 850 rbi. Maz also smacked the most famous hit in World Series history, a leadoff blast in the bottom of the ninth against the Yankees in the seventh and deciding game of the 1960 October classic.

YEARS:	17		HOME RUNS:	138
BATTING AVERAGE:	.260		RUNS BATTED IN:	853
HITS:	2,016		FIELDING AVERAGE:	.983
RUNS:	769			

VADA PINSON
Reds/Cardinals/Indians/Angels/Royals outfielder
(1958-75)

Some cynics believe that to make the Hall of Fame, you must either have been a good player in New York or the best great player on a team someplace else. If true, Pinson will enter the Hall of Fame only if he pays gate admission. Vada was overshadowed by Frank Robinson while at Cincinnati, but his lifetime numbers scream for Cooperstown enshrinement. Pinson has the most lifetime hits — 2,757 — of any player currently *not* in the Hall. He had five 200-hit seasons, socked 20 or more homers seven times, and scored 90 or more runs in nine different years. Pinson never got hurt, playing Gold Glove-caliber center field almost every day, and was considered one of the fastest men and best baserunners in the majors. Besides Pinson, only Willie Mays and Joe Morgan had at least 2,500 hits, 250 home runs, and 250 stolen bases in their big league careers.

YEARS:	18	HOME RUNS:	256
BATTING AVERAGE:	.286	RUNS BATTED IN:	1,170
HITS:	2,757	STOLEN BASES:	305
RUNS:	1,366		

LIFE AND BASEBALL

It is the best of all games for me. It frequently escapes from the pattern of the sport and assumes the form of a virile ballet. It is purer than any dance because the actions of the players are not governed by the music or crowded into a formula by a director. The movement is natural and unrehearsed and controlled only by the unexpected flight of the ball.

—Jimmy Cannon (1910–73)
sportswriter

Baseball for seven innings only is like dinner with no cognac at the end. It is like kissing the woman you love goodnight by blowing it from your fingers.

—Robert Fontaine *
"The Happy Time" (1946)

Baseball is like a poker game. Nobody wants to quit when he's losing; nobody wants you to quit when you're ahead.

—*Jackie Robinson*
Dodgers infielder (1947–56)

Baseball is like church. Many attend, but few understand.

—*Wes Westrum*
Mets manager (1965–67)

Ball teams are like human beings. They are born, live and die. Time takes care of all things.

—*Ed Barrow*
Yankees general manager (1920–45)

Baseball is a lot like life. The line drives are caught, the squibbers go for base hits. It's an unfair game.

—*Rod Kanehl*
Mets infielder (1962–64)

The box score always adds up—politics never does.

—*James Reston*
The New York Times *(1979)*

The clock doesn't matter in baseball. Time stands still or moves backward. Theoretically, one game could go on forever. Some seem to.

—Herb Caen
San Francisco Chronicle *(1979)*

Baseball is more like a novel than like a war. It is like an ongoing, hundred-year work of art, peopled with thousands of characters, full of improbable events, anecdotes, folklore and numbers.

—Luke Salisbury
The Answer Is Baseball *(1989)*

No game in the world is as tidy and dramatically neat as baseball, with cause and effect, crime and punishment, motive and result, so cleanly defined.

—Paul Gallico (1897–1976)
sportswriter

Ninety per cent of this game is half mental.

—Jim Wohlford
Brewers outfielder (1977–79)

The game has a cleanness. If you do a good job, the num-bers say so. You don't have to ask anyone or play politics. You don't have to wait for the reviews.

—Sandy Koufax
Dodgers pitcher (1955–66)

Baseball is all clean lines and clear decisions ... wouldn't life be far easier if it consisted of a series of definitive calls; safe or out, fair or foul, strike or ball. Oh, for a life like that, where every day produces a clear winner and an equally clear loser, and back to it the next day with the slate wiped clean and the teams starting out equal.

—Eric Rolfe Greenberg
The Celebrant *(1983)*

The great thing about baseball is that there's a crisis every day.

—Gabe Paul
Yankees president (1973–77)

I ain't ever had a job. I just always played baseball.

—Satchel Paige
Negro Leagues pitcher (1926–47, '55)

Satchel Paige. A man of uncommon spirit, Paige made his final big-league pitching appearance at the age of 59.

I think about baseball when I wake up in the morning. I think about it all day. And I dream about it at night. The only time I don't think about it is when I'm playing it.

—*Carl Yastrzemski*
Red Sox outfielder (1961–83)

Everyone who makes the big leagues has been a baseball standout all his life. Even so, from a big league viewpoint, he has everything to learn. It's unbelievable how much you don't know about the game you've been playing all your life.

—*Mickey Mantle*
Yankees outfielder (1951–68)

This game has taken a lot of guys over the years, who would have had to work in factories and gas stations, and made them prominent people. I only had a high school education, and believe me, I had to cheat to get that. There isn't a college in the world that would have me. And yet in this business you can walk into a room with millionaires, doctors, professional people and get more attention than they get. I don't know any other business where you can do that.

—*Sparky Anderson*
Tigers manager (1979-   )

Every time you learn something, it helps you — maybe a week, a month, maybe a year from now. Once you stop learning — let me tell you — you're going to be in the second row looking at somebody else playing.

—Ferguson Jenkins
Cubs pitcher (1966–73, '82–83)

Baseball gives you every chance to be great. Then it puts the pressure on you to prove that you haven't got what it takes. It never takes away the chance, and it never eases up on the pressure.

—Joe Garagiola
Baseball Is a Funny Game (1960)

Humanity is the keystone that holds nations and men together. When that collapses, the whole structure crumbles. This is as true of baseball teams as any other pursuit in life.

—Connie Mack
Athletics manager (1901–50)

Baseball is a game but it's more than a game. Baseball is people, dammit, and if you are around people, you can't help but get involved in their lives and care about them. And then you don't know how to talk to them or tell them how much you care and how come we know so much about pitching and we don't know squat about how to communicate? I guess that is the question.

—*Garrison Keillor*
"What Did We Do Wrong?" (1985)

I once stood outside Fenway Park in Boston, a place where the ghosts never go away, and watched a vigorous man of middle years helping, with infinite care, a frail and elderly gentleman through the milling crowds to the entry gate. Through the tears that came unexpectedly to my eyes, I saw the old man strong and important forty years before, holding the hand of a confused and excited five-year-old, showing him the way. Baseball's best moments don't always happen on the field.

—*Alison Gordon*
Foul Ball! *(1984)*

Baseball was the escape from feelings. Baseball was my relief from tension between how I felt and how my environment demanded that I act. There is no place more important in life than your hideout, and baseball was my hideout.

—*Howard Senzel*
Baseball and the Cold War *(1977)*

A true partisan will rarely switch his allegiance. The team of his childhood remains his team through good years and poor, for all the stages of his life. His style of living may vary . . . he will change jobs and even careers . . . divorce his wife and remarry . . . alter his political affiliation and social beliefs, and through it all he will continue to root for the same team he favored as a child.

—*Stanley Cohen*
The Man in the Crowd *(1981)*

Growing up is a ritual — more deadly than religion, more complicated than baseball, for there seemed to be no rules. Everything is experienced for the first time. But baseball can soothe even those pains, for it is stable and permanent, steady as a grandfather dozing in a wicker chair on a veranda.

—*W.P. Kinsella*
Shoeless Joe *(1982)*

There is magic in the moment, for when I open my eyes and see my sons in the place where my father once sat, I feel an invisible bond between our three generations, an anchor of loyalty linking my sons to the grandfather whose face they never saw but whose person they have already come to know through this most timeless of all sports, baseball.

—*Doris Kearns Goodwin*
"From Father with Love"(1987)

What's important is that baseball, after twenty-eight years of artificial turf and expansion and the designated hitter and drugs and free agency and thousand dollar bubblegum cards, is still a gift given by fathers to sons.

—*Michael Chabon*
The New York Times Magazine *(1991)*

The average American is so constructed that athletic endeavor bores him unless it is enlivened by the spirit of competition. He must be trying to "lick the other fellow" or he will quit the game in disgust. Base Ball is the one sport open to all, without any barrier of expense, and with rivalry enough to rivet the interest of its players.

—*Henry Chadwick (1824–1908)*
sportswriter

Last year, more Americans went to symphonies than went to baseball games. This may be viewed as an alarming statistic, but I think that both baseball and the country will endure.

—John F. Kennedy (1917–63)
35th President of the United States

It is designed to break your heart. The game begins in the spring, when everything else begins again, and it blossoms in the summer, filling the afternoons and evenings, and then as soon as the chill rains come, it stops and leaves you to face the fall alone.

—A. Bartlett Giamatti
"The Green Fields of the Mind" (1975)

If the human body recognized agony and frustration, people would never run marathons, have babies or play baseball.

—Carlton Fisk
Red Sox catcher (1969, '71–80)

Any time you think you have the game conquered, the game will turn around and punch you right in the nose.

—Mike Schmidt
Phillies third baseman (1972–88)

Every day is a new opportunity. You can build on yesterday's success or put its failures behind and start over again. That's the way life is, with a new game every day, and that's the way baseball is.

—*Bob Feller*
Indians pitcher (1936–41, '45–56)

You spend a good piece of your life gripping a baseball and in the end it turns out that it was the other way around all the time.

—*Jim Bouton*
Ball Four *(1970)*

Do what you love to do — and give it your very best. Whether it's business, or baseball, or the theater, or any field. If you don't love what you're doing and you can't give it your best, get out of it! Life is too short! You'll be an old man before you know it.

—*Al Lopez*
White Sox manager (1958–69)

If you're not having fun in baseball, you miss the point of everything.

—*Chris Chambliss*
Braves first baseman (1980–86)

INDEX

Special mentions of personalities are noted in italics.

Aaron, Henry, 75, 145, 342, *342*
Abell, Ferdinand, 232
Adomites, Paul, 320, 323
Allen, Dick, 65, 99, 132, 196,
    286, 330
Allen, Dwight, 21
Allen, Ethan, 95
Allen, Woody, 105
Alston, Walter, 147, 163, 343
Altrock, Nick, 333
Amalfitano, Joe, *153*
Anderson, Sparky, *43*, 56, 115,
    151, *161*, 195, 255, 314,
    322, 346, 375, 390
Andujar, Joaquin, 123, 200
Angell, Roger, 113, 233, 255,
    278, 351

Appling, Luke, *46*
Ashburn, Richie, 80, *154*, 277,
    380
Ashford, Emmett, 179
Astor, Gerald, 364

Baer, Arthur "Bugs," 275, 285
Baker, Russell, 308
Ballanfant, Lee, 178
Bamberger, George, 186
Bankhead, Tallulah, 366
Banks, Ernie, 148, 162, 344, *344*
Bannister, Alan, 348
Barber, Red, 271
Barnicle, Mike, 246
Barrow, Ed, 386
Barzun, Jacques, 18, 135, 319

Baskin, John, 275
Battey, Earl, 361
Bavasi, Buzzie, 221
Bavasi, Peter, 222
Belinsky, Bo, 236, 284
Bench, Johnny, 137, 241, 345, *345*
Berkow, Ira, 17
Berra, Yogi, 40, 53, 75, 122, 346, *346*
Bisher, Furman, 244
Bjarkman, Peter C., 265
Blair, Paul, 258
Blasingame, Don, 122
Blue, Vida, 197
Bluege, Ossie, 359
Blyleven, Bert, 128
Bodie, Ping, 358
Boone, Bob, 135, 330
Boone, Ray, 224
Boros, Steve, 60
Bosman, Dick, 334
Boswell, Thomas, 48, 51, 74, 86, 124, 151, 257, 288, 299, 317
Boudreau, Lou, 64
Bouton, Jim, 165, *208,* 215, 396

Boyd, Brendan, 183
Boyd, Brendan C., 51
Bragan, Bobby, 253, 370
Bressler, Rube, 81
Brett, George, 149
Brett, Ken, 250
Bricker, Charles, 264
Bridges, Rocky, 38, 155, 198, 378
Bridges, Tommy, 314
Briles, Nelson, 315
Brinkley, David, 275
Bristol, Dave, 150
Brock, Lou, 100, 102
Broncazio, Peter, 88
Brosnan, Jim, 165, 182, 228, 290
Broun, Heywood, 184
Brown, Bobby, 75
Brown, Joe, 303
Buhl, Bob, 40
Bulger, Boseman, 285
Bunning, Jim, 122
Burdette, Lew, 118
Burke, Michael, 14
Burke, Tim, 243
Burnett, W.R., 50

Busby, Steve, 42
Bush, George, 319

Caen, Herb, 290, 387
Campanella, Roy, 33, 136
Campbell, Bill, *180*
Cannon, Jimmy, 49, 239, 276, 350, 385
Caray, Harry, 29, 281
Cardenal, Jose, *153*
Carew, Rod, 249, 348, *348*
Carey, Max, 103
Carpenter, Ruly, 221
Carson, Johnny, 280
Cartwright, Alexander, 86
Cash, Norm, 185
Cashen, Frank, 114, 164
Caudill, Bill, 126
Cepeda, Orlando, 354
Chabon, Michael, 394
Chadwick, Henry, 88, 394
Chambliss, Chris, 396
Chance, Frank, 159
Chapman, Ray, *338*
Charboneau, Joe, 30
Cheever, John, 19
Chylak, Nestor, 175

Clark, Tom, 105
Clemens, Roger, 118, *119*
Clemente, Roberto, 58, 351, *351*
Cobb, Ty, 47, 74, 101, 140, *141*, 155, 185, 349, *349*, 358, 376
Cohane, Tim, 133
Cohen, Stanley, 20, 42, 61, 212, 393
Cohn, Lowell, 22, 61
Coleman, Jerry, 170
Coleman, Vince, 103
Conley, Gene, 335
Connors, Chuck, 336
Conroy, Pat, 210
Considine, Bob, 378
Cooper, Walker, 331
Coover, Robert, 66, 210
Corbett, Brad, 231
Cosell, Howard, 156
Cotto, Henry, *153*
Coveleski, Stanley, 146
Craig, Roger, 308
Crawford, Henry "Shag," 178
Crawford, Sam, 350
Creamer, Robert, 35

Cronin, Joe, 37, 157
Cuomo, Mario, 20
Curran, William, 87, 92
Curtis, John, 169

Daley, Arthur, 211, 344, 371,
    377
Dalton, Harry, 30, 345
Daly, Dan, 302
Dark, Alvin, 128, 157, 200, 273
Darwin, Danny, 230
Davis, Ron, 257
Davis, Willie, 146, 229
Dean, Dizzy, 118, 214, *313,*
    352, *352,* 368
Demier, Bob, 242
Dickey, Bill, 96, 134
Dickey, Glenn, 49
DiMaggio, Joe, 58, 198, *199,*
    330, 353, *353*
Doerr, Bobby, 145
Dorfman, H.A., 99
Dressen, Charlie, 159
Drysdale, Don, 127, 187, 232,
    271, 354, *354*
Durocher, Leo, 93, 140, 149,
    167, 181, 182, 185, 272

Durso, Joseph, 17
Dykes, Jimmie, 158, 163, 181
Dykstra, Len, 186

Eagleton, Thomas, 286
Eckersley, Dennis, 142
Edison, Thomas, 35
Edler, Dave, 93
Ehmke, Howard, 116
Einstein, Charles, *205,* 241
Eisenhardt, Roy, 147
Eisenhower, Dwight D., 42, *269*
Ellsworth, Dick, 335
Erskine, Carl, 367
Evers, Crabbe, 63, 193
Evers, Johnny, *44,* 56, 175, 195

Falls, Joe, 253
Farrell, James T., 302
Feather, William, 53
Feller, Bob, 135, 144, *154,* 189,
    258, 307, 308, 312, 396
Ferrara, Al, 52
Fiffer, Steve, 101
Fimrite, Ron, 260
Finley, Charles O., 92, 169, 304
Fireovid, Steve, 57

Fisk, Carlton, 14, 395
Fitzgerald, Ray, 318, 363
Flanagan, Mike, 171, 188, 261
Fontaine, Robert, 385
Ford, Whitey, 186, 236
Forster, Terry, 239
Foster, George, 84
Fox, Nellie, 364
Foxx, Jimmie, 355, *355*
Frank, Stanley, 114
Franklin, Pete, 29, 92, 202, 239
Frazier, George, 188
Fregosi, Jim, 232
Frisch, Frankie, 164
Froemming, Bruce, 177
Frommer, Harvey, 272
Frost, Robert, 115
Fuentes, Tito, 241
Fuller, Samuel, 373
Fullerton, Hugh, 98
Furillo, Carl, 78, 96
Furlong, Bill, 344

Galbraith, John Kenneth, 53
Gallego, Mike, 87
Gallico, Paul, 387
Gammons, Peter, 190, 214, 251

Garagiola, Joe, 63, 101, 132,
    137, 212, 274, 276, 321,
    337, 367, 391
Gardner, Billy, 168
Garland, Wayne, 225
Garver, Ned, 318
Garvey, Steve, 28
Gehrig, Lou, *339, 340*
Geiberger, Al, 305
Geist, Bill, 41
Gent, Peter, 66
Giamatti, A. Bartlett, 172, 395
Gibson, Bob, 96, 142, 321, 356,
    357
Gibson, Josh, 229
Goddard, Joe, 275
Goetz, Larry, 176
Golenbock, Peter, 93
Gomez, Lefty, *44,* 81, 331, 355,
    356, 371
Gomez, Preston, 170
Gooden, Dwight, 124
Goodwin, Doris Kearns, 394
Gordon, Alison, 83, 266, 392
Gorman, Tom, 178
Goslin, Goose, 23
Gossage, Rich "Goose," 153

Grant, Jim "Mudcat," 203
Graves, Louis, 304
Green, Paul M., 50
Greenberg, Eric Rolfe, 316, 388
Greenberg, Hank, 186, 198
Greenwald, Hank, 91, 270
Grey, Zane, 67
Grich, Bobby, 225, 241
Grieve, Tom, 37
Grimes, Tom, 335
Grimm, Charlie, 52
Groat, Dick, 355
Groh, Heinie, 322
Gross, Milton, 370
Grove, Lefty, 23
Guerrero, Pedro, 197
Gumbel, Bryant, 305
Gutman, Dan, 189, 300

Halberstam, David, 18
Hall, Donald, 25, 353
Hano, Arnold, 54, 121, 261, 321, 363
Hargrove, Mike, 252
Harper, Terry, *152*
Harper, Tommy, 103, 194
Harrah, Toby, 215

Harrelson, Ken, 305
Harris, Fred C., 51
Harwell, Ernie, 16, 28, 173, 254
Hebner, Richie, 303, 374
Hemingway, Ernest, 354
Henderson, Rickey, 103
Henrich, Tommy, 88
Hernandez, Keith, 64, 137, 198, 238
Hersh, Phil, 21, 203
Hershiser, Orel, 118, 322
Herskowitz, Mickey, 375
Herzog, Whitey, 90, 157, 171, 263
Higbe, Kirby, 117, 129, 185
Higgins, George V., 246
Hill, Art, 49, 54, 97, 213
Hill, Marc, *154*
Hirdt, Steve, 215
Hirshberg, Al, 368
Hoak, Don, 334
Hodges, Gil, 366, *381*
Holmes, Tommy, 372
Holway, John, 130
Honig, Donald, 95, 323, 347, 359
Hoover, Herbert, 17

Hope, Bob, 146, 270
Hornsby, Rogers, 27, 184, 305
House, Tom, 90, 120, 195, 238
Hovley, Steve, 123
Howard, Frank, 79
Hoyt, Waite, 136, 276
Hrabosky, Al, 45
Hubbard, Cal, 177
Hubbell, Carl, 45
Hugo, Richard, 41
Humphries, Rolph, 59
Hunter, Tom, 36
Hurst, Bruce, 149
Hutchinson, Fred, 167

Irvin, Monte, 308, 314
Izenberg, Jerry, 29

Jackson, Alvin, 116
Jackson, Bo, 301
Jackson, Jesse, 369
Jackson, Joe, 339
Jackson, Reggie, 56, 76, 227, 322
James, Bill, 65, 115, 211, 252,
    256, 266, 377
Jeffcoat, Hal, 329
Jenkins, Bruce, 251, 257, 278

Jenkins, Dan, 49, 193
Jenkins, Ferguson, 391
Jennings, Hughie, 162
Jessel, George, 362
Johnson, Alex, 84
Johnson, Dave, 166, 191
Johnson, Ernie, 343
Johnson, Lyndon B., 268
Johnson, Walter, 128, 358, 358
Johnstone, Jay, 165, 182, 250
Judge, Joe, 258

Kaat, Jim, 382
Kahn, Roger, 22, 267, 281
Kaline, Al, 57
Kanehl, Rod, 386
Keillor, Garrison, 392
Keller, Charlie, 45
Kelly, Mike "King," 223
Kennedy, John F., 324, 395
Kennedy, Terry, 79
Kerfeld, Charlie, 127
Kern, Jim, 231, 252
Killebrew, Harmon, 359, 359
Kiner, Ralph, 314
Kingman, Dave, 84, 152
Kinnamon, Bill, 181

Kinsella, W.P., 298, 393
Kittle, Ron, 237
Klem, Bill, 176
Klinkowitz, Jerry, 273
Kluszewski, Ted, 81, 365
Kluttz, Clyde, *219*
Knight, Ray, 143
Koenig, Mark, 372
Koppett, Leonard, 30, 89, 98,
    155, 301
Koufax, Sandy, 31, 126, 129,
    360, 361, *361,* 388
Krich, John, 19, 262, 289, 319
Kroc, Ray, 289
Kuehl, Karl, 99
Kuenn, Harvey, 256
Kuhn, Bowie, 306
Kurkjian, Tim, 244

Laga, Mike, *153*
Lamb, David, 315
Lamp, Dennis, *154*
Lancaster, Dale, 363
Lane, Frank, 130, 225
Lardner, Ring, 193, 358
LaRussa, Tony, 90
Lasorda, Tommy, 145, 162, 170

Lau, Charlie, 82, 133
Law, Vance, 78
Law, Vernon, 142
Lawson, Earl, 192
Leavy, Jane, 67, 252, 267
Lee, Bill, 188, 247, 260, 310
Lefebvre, Jim, 64
Lemon, Bob, 39, 125, 237
Leonard, Buck, 229, 368
Leonard, John, 301
Lewis, Joe E., 260
Leyland, Jim, 31, 228
Leyva, Nick, 202
Lieb, Fred, 376
Liebling, A.J., 259
Loes, Billy, 147
Logan, Bob, 250
Lolich, Mickey, 31
Lombardi, Ernie, 310
Lonborg, Jim, 303
Long, Dale, 74
Lopat, Ed, 116
Lopez, Al, 160, 168, 396
Lopez, Hector, 346
Lowenstein, John, 216
Lowry, Philip, 255
Luciano, Ron, 125, 131, 178

Lurie, Bob, 229
Lyle, Sparky, 125, 332
Lyons, Ted, 356

Mack, Connie, 350, 391
Madden, Bill, 323
Madlock, Bill, 285, 290
Maglie, Sal, *43*, 127
Malamud, Bernard, *204*, 337
Maloney, Jim, 346
Mantegna, Joe, 345
Mantle, Mickey, 38, 62, 362,
    362, 364, 390
Maranville, Rabbit, 239
Maris, Roger, 220
Marquard, Rube, 235
Martin, Billy, 158, 184, 230, 243,
    259
Martin, Pepper, 352
Mathewson, Christy, 30, 143,
    174
Mauch, Gene, *45*, 148, 149, 168,
    362
Maye, Lee, 80
Mays, Willie, 39, 79, 142, 365,
    365, 370
Mazeroski, Bill, *383*

McCarthy, Joe, 91
McCarver, Tim, 78, 137, 201,
    251, 317, 357
McDowell, Sam, 121
McGraw, John, 159, 222, 376
McGraw, Tug, 39
McKeon, Jack, 159, 223
McLain, Denny, 236, 254
Messersmith, Andy, 214
Michaels, Al, 47
Miller, Francis Trevelyan, 18
Miller, Ray, 27, 188
Minton, Greg, 35
Mize, Johnny, 307
Monroe, Marilyn, *199*
Morgan, Joe, 100
Morris, Jack, 197
Morris, Willie, 370
Munson, Thurman, 23
Murphy, Dale, 82
Murray, Jim, 28, 37, 60, 234,
    247, 249, 279, 287, 289,
    375
Murtaugh, Danny, 48
Musial, Stan, 76, 187, 366, *366*

Nelson, Dave, 104

Nettles, Graig, 230, 262
Neudecker, Jerry, 174
Niekro, Phil, 187
Nixon, Richard, 192
North, Bill, 171, 331

O'Donnell, Bob, 302
O'Doul, Lefty, 225, 287
Oh, Sadaharu, 85
Ojeda, Bob, 57
Oliver, Al, 374
O'Malley, Walter, 190, 220
Ostler, Scott, 156
Ott, Mel, 347
Owens, Paul, 159

Paige, Satchel, 122, 331, 367,
    367, 388, 389
Palmer, Peter, 16, 216
Pappas, Milt, 124
Parker, Dave, 286
Parrott, Harold, 232
Passarella, Art, 353
Paul, Gabe, 388
Pearlman, Donn, 50
Peary, Danny, 52
Peckinpaugh, Roger, 310

Pepitone, Joe, 278
Perry, Gaylord, 187, 311
Pesky, Johnny, 139
Peters, Hank, 222
Phillips, B.J., 26
Phillips, Lefty, 150
Piniella, Lou, 130
Pinson, Vada, 385
Pipgras, George, 181
Plimpton, George, 123, 304
Pope, Edwin, 26, 38, 50, 320
Postema, Pam, 136
Povich, Shirley, 312, 359
Pryor, Greg, 65
Purkey, Bob, 117

Quigley, Martin, 130, 184
Quilici, Frank, 348
Quisenberry, Dan, 90, 167, 248

Randle, Lenny, 263
Rapoport, Ron, 233
Reese, Pee Wee, 131
Reichler, Joseph, 207
Reidenbaugh, Lowell, 62
Reilly, Rick, 242
Reston, James, 386

Reuss, Jerry, 123, 290
Reynolds, Allie, 120
Reynolds, R.J., 200
Rice, Damon, 298
Rice, Grantland, 352
Richards, Paul, 20, 22, 83, 164, 361
Richler, Mordecai, 280
Rickey, Branch, 83, 99, 230, 350
Rigney, Bill, 87, 366
Ripken Jr., Cal, 245
Ritter, Lawrence, 206, 342
Ritz, David, 273
Rixey, Eppa, 80
Rizzuto, Phil, 202
Roberts, Robin, 39, 146, 157, 351
Robertson, James Oliver, 13
Robinson, Brooks, 32, 44, 236, 337
Robinson, Frank, 100, 139, 165, 251, 311, 312
Robinson, Jackie, 94, 369, 369, 386
Robinson, Wilbert, 166
Rodgers, Buck, 282
Rogers, Will, 324

Rooker, Jim, 240
Rooney, Andy, 54, 95, 215
Rose, Pete, 23, 33, 102, 140, 166, 228, 231, 332, 357
Roseboro, John, 336
Rosen, Al, 14, 84
Rosen, Alan, 51
Rosenbaum, Art, 179
Roth, Philip, 35
Rothschild, Larry, 122
Royko, Mike, 261
Rue, Joe, 174
Ruffing, Red, 353
Ruppert, Jacob, 140
Rust, Art, 16, 173
Ruth, Babe, 35, 196, 226, 227, 240, 274, 333, 349, 371, 371
Ryan, Nolan, 126, 144
Ryba, Mike, 224

Salisbury, Luke, 21, 213, 299, 387
Santarone, Pat, 64
Sawyer, Eddie, 156
Sax, Steve, 152
Sayles, John, 120

Schecter, Leonard, 150, 208, 260

Scheinblum, Richie, 253

Schmidt, Mike, 282, *283,* 395

Scott, George, 79

Scully, Vin, 214, 329, 357

Seaver, Tom, 139, 190

Senzel, Howard, 74, 191, 212, 393

Shannon, Mike, 355

Shantz, Bobby, 336, 378

Shaughnessy, Dan, 248

Sheed, Wilfrid, 14, 194, 211, 284, 300

Shepherd, Jean, 250

Sherrod, Blackie, 259, 265

Sherry, Norm, 117

Shor, Toots, 282

Sievers, Roy, 311

Simmons, Curt, 343

Simmons, Lon, 68

Simmons, Ted, 76, 196

Siwoff, Seymour, 211

Skowron, Bill, 76

Slaughter, Enos, 334

Smith, Al, 201

Smith, Mayo, 240

Smith, Ozzie, 177, 288

Smith, Red, 61, 169, 304, 365

Snider, Duke, 24, 31, 272, 309, 310, 369

Spahn, Warren, 89, 116, 121, 125, 367

Spalding, A.G., 40, 176

Spander, Art, 274, 280

Speaker, Tris, 36, 349

Spink, C.C. Johnson, 227

Stargell, Willie, 82, 332, 361, 373, *373*

Staub, Rusty, 77

Steinbeck, John, 267

Steinbrenner, George, 222, 223

Stengel, Casey, 91, 131, 134, 160, 169, *180,* 201, 237, 240, 281, 307, 334, 347, 374, *374*

Stewart, Ernie, 179

Stone, Steve, 120, 271

Street, Jim, 263

Stuart, Dick, *44*

Sugar, Bert Randolph, 268

Sutcliffe, Rick, 121, 318

Sutton, Don, 228, 374

Swift, E.M., 264

Swoboda, Ron, 329

Taft, William Howard, 183
Tanner, Chuck, 162, 373
Tebbetts, Birdie, 126, 164
Terry, Bill, 233
Thomas, Gorman, *153*, 256
Thompson, Fresco, 284
Thorn, John, 16, 36, 62, 65, 66, 130, 216
Thrift, Syd, 129, 315
Thurber, James, 52
Toma, George, 63
Torborg, Jeff, 138
Torchia, Tony, 77
Torre, Joe, 145
Truman, Harry S, 173
Tunis, John R., 191
Turley, Bob, 38
Turner, Ted, 148, 221

Uecker, Bob, 133, 172, 284
Updike, John, 247, 330, 379

Vance, Sandy, 333
Vanderberg, Bob, 249
Vander Meer, Johnny, 33, 58

Van Slyke, Andy, 148, 229
Vaughn, Bill, 67, 277
Veale, Bob, 114
Vecsey, George, 27, 192, 372
Veeck, Bill, 47, 48, 185, 223, 300, 306
Verdi, Bob, 246
Vertlieb, Dick, 264
Virdon, Bill, 160

Wagner, Honus, 376, *376*
Wagner, Leon, 57
Wallopp, Douglass, 41
Walls, Lee, 235
Walsh, Ed, 115
Walters, Bucky, 197
Waner, Paul, 56
Ward, John Montgomery, 221
Weatherby, W.J., 19
Weaver, Earl, 29, 89, 113, 156, 160, 167, 182, 299
Weiss, George, 194
Weiss, Walt, 89
Wendelstedt, Harry, 175
Westrum, Wes, 386
Wheeler, Lonnie, 275, 343
Whicker, Mark, 279

White, Frank, 309
Whitman, Walt, 13
Wilhelm, Hoyt, 132
Will, George, 19, 144, 175, 274
Williams, Billy, 77
Williams, Dick, 158, 281, 288, 309
Williams, Edward Bennett, 233, 299
Williams, Ted, 24, 72, 73, 76, 78, 80, 82, 168, 200, 365, 377, 377
Wills, Maury, 102, 104, 163, 213
Wilson, Earl, 40
Wilson, Hack, 238
Wilson, Willie, 101
Winfield, Dave, 75, 143, 189, 224

Wodehouse, P.G., 320
Wohlford, Jim, 291, 387
Wolfe, Thomas, 26, 72, 287
Wood, Bob, 68, 248, 254, 262, 264, 266, 277
Wright, Craig R., 104, 134, 265
Wrigley, P.K., 170, 220
Wynn, Early, 129
Wynn, Jimmy, 46, 279

Yastrzemski, Carl, 333, 390
Young, Dick, 231
Young, Geoffrey, 86
Youngman, Henny, 53

Zinsser, William, 27, 32, 66

ABOUT THE AUTHOR

David Plaut is literary critic for *USA Today Baseball Weekly*. He is the author of *Start Collecting Baseball Cards, Baseball Wit and Wisdom,* and a forthcoming book on the Dodgers–Giants pennant race of 1962.

Plaut is also an Emmy award-winning writer and director with NFL Films. He has produced three of the best-selling sports videos of all time, as well as programs for the major networks, HBO, and ESPN. Plaut lives with his wife and son in Moorestown, New Jersey.